HISTORIC HERALDRY OF BRITAIN

1274   1329
ROBERT BRUCE.
KING OF SCOTLAND.

HISTORIC HERALDRY OF BRITAIN

AN ILLUSTRATED SERIES OF BRITISH HISTORICAL ARMS, WITH NOTES, GLOSSARY, AND AN INTRODUCTION TO HERALDRY

BY
SIR ANTHONY WAGNER
K.C.V.O., D.LITT., F.S.A.

Garter Principal King of Arms

PHILLIMORE
LONDON and CHICHESTER

First published in 1939 by
OXFORD UNIVERSITY PRESS
Second Impression, 1948

This reprint published by
PHILLIMORE & CO. LTD.
Shopwyke Hall, Chichester, Sussex, England
1972

ISBN 0 85033 022 X

Text printed by Fletcher & Son Ltd., Norwich
Plates printed on Ambassador Art 160gsm paper by
Eyre & Spottiswoode Ltd., Her Majesty's Printers, at
Grosvenor Press, Portsmouth

PREFACE

In January, 1938, being then a junior Pursuivant (Portcullis) at the College of Arms, I was asked to produce a scheme of heraldic decoration for the British Pavilion at the projected New York World's Fair which was to open in March, 1939. This ultimately took the form of a series of paintings for the ante-room illustrating phases of British History by heraldic symbolism, a pedigree decorated with shields of Arms showing the descent of George Washington from a number of the Barons Sureties of Magna Carta to accompany the Magna Carta original, which was brought from England and displayed, and a series of the Arms of one hundred and forty two outstanding figures from the history of England, Scotland, Ireland and Wales, which formed the decoration of a great hall. The present book is based on the last of these series which consisted of one hundred and twenty eight modelled and coloured shields, each some three feet high, and fourteen larger armorial achievements each some nine feet high, representing leading historical figures of successive centuries. The large panels were carried out by Mr. Gilbert Bayes and the smaller shields by Mr. Cecil Thomas, all from designs by Mr. Gerald Cobb, Herald Painter at the College of Arms, under my direction. In the selection of the historical figures I had the help of my old and dear friend Professor V. H. Galbraith.

As those who will recall those years will understand, there was a moment when political events made it doubtful whether the pavilion would open at all, but it did and I was in New York for its opening, though following the ensuing Declaration of War the shields were not brought back to England but were presented by the British Government to the United States Government. The sixteen large panels were given to the Metropolitan Museum of Arts, New York, where it was planned to use them as decorative and illustrative material in the installation of the Armour Galleries. However, owing to the evacuation of the Museum during the war, this installation was never completed, and when the Museum's collections were returned the entire distribution system of the galleries was rearranged, so that there was no place for these. The panels were then transferred to the J. A. Schuller Museum in Rochester, New Hampshire, where they were installed in 1951.

Meanwhile, the modelled and painted Shields were given to the Library of Congress and by them in the 1960's to the Smithsonian Institution, Washington. The Smithsonian passed on approximately half of them to the National Cathedral for use in the St. Alban's Preparatory School for Boys in Washington, where they are now on display in the offices and classrooms in good condition and well maintained. The Shields and panels remaining in the Smithsonian, however, are for the most part in storage, though some twenty are on display in the Smithsonian Institution Building in the Commons or dining room for staff and distinguished guests.

I remember the months of preparation as a hectic sequence of research, of discussion of the plan with the architect Mr. Howard Robertson and with Sir Louis Beale, Commissioner General for His Majesty's Government for the New York World's Fair, and of rapid oscillation between the studios of Mr. Gerald Cobb, Mr. Gilbert Bayes and Mr. Cecil Thomas, supervising and, with the rashness of youth, criticizing their beautiful productions as these grew under their hands and those of their assistants.

The book has long been out of print and I would express my gratitude to the Oxford University Press for now permitting it to be republished by Phillimore & Company. This being a reprint, I have not attempted to rewrite the book or introduce new material, but I may here mention that the brief list of Rolls of Arms on pages 25 - 31 is the forerunner of my book *A Catalogue of British Mediaeval Rolls of Arms,* which was published jointly by the Society of Antiquaries and the Harleian Society in 1950, as the first volume of a series entitled *Aspilogia.* Some revisions of this Catalogue were incorporated in the second volume of *Aspilogia* published in 1967.

Anthony Wagner, Garter

ACKNOWLEDGMENTS

to the First and Second Impressions

The publisher desires to express his gratitude to the Commissioner-General for His Majesty's Government in the United Kingdom for the permission to illustrate this book with reproductions of the heraldic reliefs carried out for the British Pavilion at the New York World's Fair by Mr. Gilbert Bayes (the large panels shown in Plates I, V, VI, X, XI, XIV, XV, XVIII, XIX, XXII, XXV, are his) and Mr. Cecil Thomas (the shields in the remaining Plates are his), from designs by Mr. Gerald Cobb, under Mr. Wagner's direction.

The author wishes to thank Professor V. H. Galbraith, Mr. Oswald Barron, F.S.A., Maltravers Herald Extraordinary, Mr. S. M. Collins, F.S.A., and the many others (some of them named in the text) who have given him valuable help.

The issue of the present reprint of 500 copies only has made it possible to undertake a limited revision of the text. The author is obliged to several friends for pointing out errors and omissions, but especially to Mr. W. H. Humphreys, F.S.A., and Mr. E. A. Greening Lamborn, F.S.A.

NOTE ON CONTENTS

This list indicates the positioning of the illustrations in this new edition:

CONTENTS

NOTES ON THE SERIES OF HISTORICAL ARMS

*

CORRIGENDA

The author is obliged to several friends for pointing out errors and omissions, but especially to Mr. W. A. Humphreys, F.S.A., and Mr. E. A. Greening Lamborn, F.S.A. It has been possible to make some of these corrections in the text: others are given below and are denoted by an asterisk in the text.

Page 20, line 1. The definition of heir and coheir is incomplete. After 'brothers' should be added, 'and her father is dead'. In line 3, after 'only', insert '(or if, through extinction of all issue of brothers, their mother or remoter ancestress has become, whether in her lifetime or *in her issue*, heir or coheir to her father)'.

Page 24, note 1. Add a Catalogue of English Mediaeval Rolls of Arms by the present writer, to be published by the Society of Antiquaries and the Harleian Society should before long supersede this.

Page 28 (XVIII) GRIMALDI'S ROLL. Most of the middle section of the Roll, Nos. 43-127, are taken from Glover's Roll.

Page 35, line 11. The text of Glover's Roll edited by Nicolas has 'Le Banner party endentee d'argent et de goules' while the window at Chartres shows the banner gules and *argent*.

Pages 36-7 No. 4. Mr. R. B. Haselden of the Huntingdon Library, California, told the writer of a seal of Strongbow there formerly at Stowe. A note on this by the writer appeared in the Antiquaries' Journal, Vol. 21, pp. 128-132. The obverse shows an equestrian figure with a non-armorial shield, the counterseal a standing figure with javelin and shield of six chevrons, as in that of Earl Gilbert.

Page 38. No. 5. Fulk Fitzwarin (living 1250), whose descendants bore *Quarterly indented argent and gules*, married Maud widow of Theobald Walter and hence probably derived his arms—but possibly from his second marriage with Clarice d'Auberville.

Page 50. line 7. Though the blazon in the Parliamentary Roll is *quartele dargent et de sable*, it should read not *sable* but *gules*, and is always so given elsewhere.

Page 55. No. 42. The note needs correction. The coat *Argent a chief gules a lion rampant over all* is that of Burghersh of Ewelme, Oxfordshire, whose heiress Maud (d.1437) married Thomas Chaucer the poet's son. Anthony Wood noted arms in an ancient window in Woodstock church of Chaucer *Party argent and gules a bend counterchanged* impaling Burghersh of Ewelme, with crest *A unicorn's head argent out of a coronet or* (Harleian Society, Vol. 5, p. 53, information from Mr. E. A. Greening Lamborn, F.S.A.). A seal of Thomas Chaucer with shield *Party a bend* and crest *A unicorn's head* is recorded in a 17th century manuscript in the possession of Dr. Harold Bowditch, F.S.A. The Burghersh coat is attributed to *Tomas Chawserys* in MS Harl. 2169 fo. 58b (Ancestor No. 9, p. 165: Foster, Two Tudor Books of Arms, p. 94), appears on his tomb at Ewelme (with his mother's arms of Roet) to the exclusion of his paternal coat and was so quartered by the son of his daughter and heir, John de la Pole, Duke of Suffolk (window at Ockwells, Berkshire). A seal on a deed of 1363, in the Record Office, of John Chaucer, vintner of London, presumably Geoffrey's father, show arms *Ermine on a chief three birds' heads*.

Page 60. No. 51. ARMS OF THE SEE OF CANTERBURY. Everard Green, Rouge Dragon, argued convincingly (Proceedings of the Society of Antiquaries, 2nd Series, Vol. XVI. page 394) that the cross and pall device, now used as the arms of the Archbishoprics of Canterbury, Dublin and Armagh, and formerly also that of York, was originally simply that of an Archbishop. The distinctive coat of the *church* of Canterbury was that now used by the Dean, *Azure on a cross argent the Greek letters Chi and Iota in pale in black letter*. This appears on the seals of Cardinal Pole and Archbishops Cranmer and Parker and under the arms of Chicheley in the Chicheley porch.

Page 62. No. 55. Later information from Mr. John H. Harvey, F.S.A., shows that the musician cannot be identical with John Dunstable of Bradfield and Steeple Morden, who made his will in 1459. They may however have been kinsmen.

Page 93, No. 119. See further the 'Pedigree of Austen' by R. A. Austen-Leigh, privately printed 1940, where the genealogical evidence here given is more fully set out.

Page 100, No. 135. J. W. Mackail in 'The Life of William Morris', 1899, Vol. I pp. 11-12, writes "For a number of years before his death Mr. Morris had held a position of some consequence in the district, and was a well known name in the City. In 1843 he obtained a grant of arms from the Heralds' College: 'Azure a horse's head erased argent between three horse shoes or, and for crest, on a wreath of the colours, a horse's head couped argent, charged with three horse shoes in chevron sable.' The boy of nine was already of an age to be keenly interested in heraldry; and whatever may have been the reasons which induced Garter and Clarenceux to assign these bearings, they became in his mind something deeply, if obscurely, associated with his life. He considered himself in some sense a tribesman of the White Horse. In the house which he built for himself afterwards the horse's head is pictured on tiles and glass painted by his own hand. To the White Horse of the Berkshire downs, which lies within a drive of his later home at Kelmscott, he made a regular yearly pilgrimage".

HISTORICAL NOTE

The following pages describe, document and explain the Arms of one hundred and forty two outstanding figures from the history of England, Scotland, Ireland and Wales. An historian glancing down the list will probably at once be struck with points which seem to him to call for explanation. Why is this name included, while that more eminent is left out? Is not the proportion of men of this kind too high, of those of that too low? These and other questions can be best answered by a short account of the way in which the names were chosen.

It was decided, first of all, to group them by centuries and, so far as possible, to give each century equal representation. This meant giving the Middle Ages a larger share than probably they would otherwise have had. But of this, students of Heraldry, at any rate, will not complain, for it is to the Middle Ages that the origin, fullest development and finest examples of their science belong. Its first appearance in the second quarter of the twelfth century gave us our earlier limit, and the decision to include no living person our later. Between them our list falls into seven sections; the first and last comprising each a century and a bit, and containing twenty six names apiece; the rest a century each with eighteen names. From each section two outstanding figures were chosen for more elaborate treatment than the rest. For the first three, that is, the Mediæval centuries, our illustrations show these chosen subjects as mounted figures in full armour displaying Heraldry on shields, coats, banners and horse trappers. For the modern centuries, the place of these is taken by full achievements of Arms, complete with Supporters. The figures treated in this way have necessarily been, for the first three centuries knights and not, for instance, churchmen, and for the last three peers or belonging to one of the other categories entitled to Supporters. For the remainder shields only (without crests) are described and illustrated.

Our list had therefore to comprise one hundred and forty-two names representing as fully as possible all aspects of the national history and achievement. In addition Arms had to be provable for them all. We decided that the

B

9

right procedure was first to draw up a list on purely historical grounds, and then to apply heraldic research to it.

The first step, though relatively simple, threatened to be laborious—the extraction, namely, of a short list from the Dictionary of National Biography. We were, however, fortunate in finding that a great part of this work had been done for us some years since by Dr. Havelock Ellis in his book *A Study of British Genius*,[1] in which, 'by means of a slightly complicated and so far as possible objective method of selection', which is explained at length, he drew up a list of one thousand and thirty 'persons of preeminent intellectual ability' respecting whom biographical details adequate for his purpose were forthcoming.

From Dr. Ellis' list of 1030 names I selected about 200 of the most eminent, but omitting those whom I already knew to be non-armigerous. Dr. Ellis' list, however, being, from the manner of its compilation, somewhat weak in Mediaeval names, a number of these were added by selection from Stubbs' Constitutional History. At this point I was able to enlist the valuable help of Professor V. H. Galbraith of the University of Edinburgh, and to him the list thus formed was submitted. He, after making small additions, selected the requisite number of names. Research was then undertaken to see if Arms could be found for all of them. For the Mediæval period contemporary evidence that the Arms had in fact been used was required; for the modern period record of Arms for the family in question by official heraldic authority (see pp. 20-23).

The results of passing eminence through this heraldic sieve were of much interest and will be examined shortly. A consequence of the arrangement by centuries may, however, be mentioned first. This is, that, achievement being distributed unevenly through the centuries of our history, the average level of eminence in sixteen men picked from any one century will not necessarily tally with that of the rest. In fact our choice in some centuries was made as hard by the superfluity of eminence, as in others by its dearth. The problems of the earliest section more than once provoked my coadjutor to echo the sad comment of Professor Tout on certain feudal lords that they are, after all, for the historian 'as like each other as a row of peas'. We had further to try to keep a just balance between eminence of different kinds, between writers and men of action, saints and artists, with the result that in the sixteenth century, for instance, some writers of great eminence had to be left out because their class was already so well represented.

[1] Constable & Company, Ltd., 1927.

It might be thought that the heraldic criterion would produce a list of men more notable for noble blood than for personal achievements. The briefest inspection, however, shows that this is not so, and it is of interest to consider why. The first reason is that while Arms have indeed been used and granted as a mark of nobility, nobility in this context means, and in England has always meant, what we should more usually call gentility. Secondly, this class of the nobility or gentry has in England never been a fixed or rigid class into which entry was unduly difficult. As Stubbs puts it, 'The great peculiarity of the baronial state in England as compared with the continent, is the absence of the idea of caste: the English lords do not answer to the nobles of France, or to the princes and counts of Germany, because in our system the theory of the nobility of blood as conveying political privilege has no legal recognition. English nobility is merely the nobility of the hereditary counsellors of the crown, the right to give counsel being involved at one time in the tenure of land, at another in the fact of summons, at another in the terms of a patent; it is the result rather than the cause of peerage. The nobleman is the person who for his life holds the hereditary office denoted or implied in his title. The law gives to his children and kinsmen no privilege which it does not give to the ordinary freeman, unless we regard certain acts of courtesy, which the law has recognized, as implying privilege.'[1]

Among the consequences of this system is a long-established fluidity in our social distinctions. For knights' sons to be apprenticed to trades and knight-hoods to be conferred on citizens has been rather the rule than the exception. That the use of the traditional symbol of gentility should, in spite of this, be tenaciously continued, is perhaps not less characteristic.

We are apt to think of Arms as essentially ancient, or at least as interesting in proportion to their antiquity, and thus to overlook the fact that old Coats no less than new ones have had their beginning. Of our present list we shall find that a large proportion were the first, or nearly the first, of their respective families to bear Arms. In the Mediaeval period this is less easily demon-strable, yet the following appear to be the first known bearers of their several Coats—Geoffrey de Mandeville, Ranulph de Glanville, Geoffrey fitz Piers, William the Marshal, Falkes de Bréauté, Hubert de Burgh, Walter de Merton, Robert Burnel, Sir John Hawkwood, Geoffrey Chaucer, William of Wykeham, Sir John Oldcastle, Richard Whittington, Henry Chicheley, John Dunstable and John Fisher. While in the modern period the following were either Grantees or the sons of Grantees of Arms—John Colet, Sir Thomas

1 'The Constitutional History of England', Oxford. 2nd Edition, 1867, Vol. II, pp. 176-7

More, Thomas Cromwell, Thomas Cranmer, Sir Francis Drake, William
Shakespeare, Sir John Hawkins, Francis Bacon, William Laud, John Win-
throp, William Harvey, John Milton, Sir Richard Arkwright, Lord Nelson,
Samuel Taylor Coleridge, George Stephenson, Lord Macaulay, Lord Beaconsfield, Lord Tennyson, William Morris, William Ewart Gladstone, John
Ruskin, Lord Lister, Lord Kelvin, Lord Kitchener, and Lord Rutherford.
A class within this list worth further analysis is that of men belonging to what
may be called the second generation of wealth, and deriving from advantages
of education owed to their fathers' efforts much of the special character of
their genius and achievement.

On the other side attention may be drawn to the relatively rare occurrence,
in this series, of really ancient Coats. The eighteenth century, with five out of
eighteen dating from the fourteenth, is exceptional. The same century is
remarkable also for the only two groups of a father and son—the Walpoles
and the Pitts. The cousinship of Horace Walpole on one side with Nelson
(No. 117), on another with Dryden and Swift,[1] and on a third with Lord
Chesterfield, is particularly noteworthy. Nor should the exalted station of an
earlier family group be allowed to obscure the exceptional natural gifts of its
members. I refer to the male line of our old Royal House, including three
kings of extraordinary brilliance—Edward I, Edward III, and Henry V,
who as sovereigns are excluded from the present list—the Black Prince, John
of Gaunt, the Dukes of Bedford and Gloucester, Cardinal Beaufort and Lady
Margaret Beaufort, as well as the more accidentally eminent Richard, King of
the Romans.

The list of those who had to be omitted because they had no Arms, was
shorter than might have been expected, yet it did to our regret include several
names of the first eminence, and especially in the three categories of painters,
philosophers, and religious leaders. The arts are represented indeed by Wren,
William Morris and Ruskin; but Hogarth, Reynolds, Romney, Gains-
borough, Girtin, Cotman, Constable and Turner, to name no more, are non-
armigerous.[2] Reynolds, indeed, belongs to the tantalising class of those who
used Arms but without apparent right. The Coat he used belonged to the
Reynolds family of Langport, Somerset, and Melcombe Regis, Dorset,

[1] W. T. J. Gun, 'Studies in Hereditary Ability', 1928, pp. 123-127.
[2] Compare Havelock Ellis' conclusion (A Study of British Genius, p. 73) that 'painters and sculptors constitute a group which appears to be of very distinct interest from the point of view of occupa-
tional heredity. In social origin, it may be noted, the group differs strikingly in constitution from the
general body in which the upper class is almost or quite predominant. Of 63 painters and sculptors
of definitely known origin, only two can be placed in the aristocratic division.'

whereas his own family so far back as it has been traced is found in the immediate neighbourhood of Exeter. Of the philosophers Roger Bacon was of a knightly house, but no connection with any of the knights of the name whose Arms are known, has been established. Nothing is known of the antecedents of William of Ockham or Duns Scotus. Locke apparently used Arms, but by no right that I can discover. Berkeley was possibly of Lord Berkeley's kin, but the pedigree is unproved. Hume never matriculated as a cadet in Lyon's Register and therefore remains non-armigerous, though the chief of his house had matriculated. Francis Bacon, therefore, stands alone for British philosophy. The saddest gaps among the religious leaders are left by John Knox, to whom Lord Ranfurly's Arms are sometimes attributed without apparent justification; John Wesley, who has been provided with a lengthy pedigree, but, alas, untenable; Keble; and Newman. Among poets, the chief omissions are perhaps Spenser (for want of proof of his pedigree); Pope; Blake; Wordsworth (who used Arms which seem to be apocryphal); Keats; and Browning. Among the writers of prose, Bunyan, Dr. Johnson, and Dickens; among inventors, Caxton (who may, however, be an armigerous Causton); and Faraday; among musicians, Byrd, whose Arms were entered at a Visitation but without colours; and Purcell, who probably was of the family of Purcell of Onslow whose Arms he used, but is not yet proved to be so; and of others, most regrettably Florence Nightingale, who falls but one degree outside the limitations of a grant of Arms. In spite of these gaps, however, heraldry, we claim, is able to commemorate a full and representative series of British historical figures.

HERALDIC INTRODUCTION

How to Use this Book

This book is primarily a set of notes on a particular set of Shields of Arms, chosen for the historical importance of their bearers. These have, however, so wide a range in time, and between them illustrate so many aspects and problems of Heraldry, that it has seemed worth while to add an introduction and glossary which will make it possible for a reader with no previous knowledge of the subject to use the book as a primer or text book.

This he can do in two ways. He may plunge straight into the middle of the subject by opening at any shield that interests him and comparing the blazon (technical description) with the picture. This may in itself make the meaning of the terms of the blazon plain to him. If it does not, he can look up in the glossary those which defeat him. And last of all, finding there some references to this introduction, he may perhaps turn to it for a more general view of the subject.

The other way is to begin with this general view and work down to the details. The sections which follow deal with their subject matter only in the briefest and most general way and for the most part without discussion of examples or explanation of technical terms. For these, reference is made to the glossary, where in turn, under each term defined, references are given to the places of its occurrence in the notes and plates.

What is Heraldry?

Heraldry in the large sense is the whole duty of Heralds, not merely that part of it which relates to the bearing of Arms, to which this name is commonly given. Even today the English Heralds have duties of proclamation and of marshalling and taking part in ceremonies of state, as well as an official responsibility for Records of Arms and Pedigree and a professional concern in the study of all records bearing on these matters. From the fourteenth century to the sixteenth they were constantly employed as Royal Messengers in war and peace, at times even with the status of Ambassadors.

To find the link connecting these oddly assorted functions we must look back to the Middle Ages and to the institution in connection with which we first[1] find Heralds mentioned—namely the tournament. Heralds were professional criers or proclaimers. When a knight entered the lists to joust it was the Heralds' duty to recognize him and to announce his name and titles to the assembled company. From this primary duty it seems likely that all the rest developed. Soon the Heralds were made responsible for the whole conduct of tournaments and their ceremonious preliminaries, and from this it was no great step to entrust other ceremonies to them. The holding of a tournament was proclaimed by them beforehand at neighbouring courts; hence their employment as messengers. Finally, their concern with Coats of

[1] c. 1170, by Chrêtien de Troyes, Le Chevalier de la Charette, ed. Wendelin Förster, 1899, ll. 5553-5565. And see the present writer's 'Heralds and heraldry in the Middle Ages', Oxford, Clarendon Press, 1939, and 'Heraldry in England', King Penguin Books, 1946.

14

Arms almost certainly sprang from their need to recognize the knights whose titles they must proclaim. Often they could know them only by their Arms, and of Arms, therefore, they were bound to have a special and extensive knowledge.

In considering Heraldry in this narrower sense, we have first to ask, 'What is a Coat of Arms?' It is a personal and hereditary device whose nature is determined by the tapering form of the shield on which it is most characteristically displayed. Let us see what this implies.

Personal devices, like national and tribal emblems, go back to the beginnings of history. The Royal emblems of Upper and Lower Egypt, the Seal devices of the Sumerians and Greeks, the Roman Legionary standards and Red Indian Totems fall into this class. But these were not hereditary and therefore not heraldic. Only one true forerunner of mediæval Heraldry is known to me—the system of shield devices used by the great Athenian families in the sixth and fifth centuries before Christ.

The first definite evidence of Heraldry as we know it belongs to the second quarter of the twelfth century. When Henry I of England knighted his son-in-law Geoffrey of Anjou in 1127, he put round his neck a shield of golden lions (see No. 9). Not much later, equestrian figures upon seals begin to show heraldic charges on their flags and shields; and by 1150 there is evidence from this source for the use of Arms in England (see Nos. 4, 22), France, Germany, Spain and Italy. Little more than a generation earlier, the Bayeux Tapestry shows devices borne on shields and flags indeed, but irregularly and without apparent system.

So sudden and widespread a development suggests a single cause. Out of many that have been conjectured, the least unlikely are perhaps the rise of the tournament and the first crusade. Whatever its origin, this at least is plain, that heraldry's aim was conspicuous distinctiveness—and how well this was achieved our coloured plates show.

There are some slight indications that the bearing of heraldic devices upon lance flags preceded their use on shields. If so, however, the latter quickly took first place, and it is the tapering form of the thirteenth century shield that has as much as anything given Heraldry its peculiar aesthetic quality. Some writers have explained the 'ordinaries'—chevrons, bends, saltires and the rest—as, in their origin, structural bars or bands for strengthening the shield. To put the thing in this way is surely to miss the point. These particular bands and bars arise not merely from the material but, more pertinently, from the aesthetic structure of the shield. They are in fact its axes, which divide it

15

symmetrically and must therefore underlie any satisfactory pattern based on the shield form. A full analysis of the principles and practice of mediæval armorial design would be of equal value to the aesthetic theorist and the student of Heraldry. So long as this principle of balance and of the relation of charges to shield form was grasped, heraldic design flourished. And this grasp did not, as is sometimes said, wholly expire with the middle ages. The average level, indeed, declined, but the best inventions were as good, though naturally not often as simple, as formerly.

But the shield, though central, is not the whole of Heraldry. The shield device could be borne as well on the banner and horse trapper and on the surcoat (or later tabard), which has given its name—'Coat of Arms'—to heraldic bearings generally. The 'external ornaments'—Crest, Supporters and Badge —on the other hand, generally, though not always, differed in design from the shield.

The Crest, as its name implies, was a solid figure or device attached to the top of the helm. In modern times, however, it has too often been thought of merely as a flat composition on paper, and Crests have in consequence sometimes been granted which would be absurd or impossible in the round. In the present series only the large panels show Crests, Nos. 27, 28, 45, and 46 in actual use, Nos. 64, 71, 72, 89, 90, 107 and 108 in Achievements of Arms— that is to say, upon helmets surmounting shields. From the helmet hangs mantling (q.v.) designed to protect the wearer from the sun's heat. Special shapes and positions of helmet (q.v.) to distinguish the bearer's rank date only from James I's reign, and the distinctive patterns of coronet (q.v.) about half a century earlier, though coronets were worn by dukes to mark their dignity as early as the reign of Edward III.

Supporters (q.v.)—that is, the figures of living creatures placed on either side of the shield as though to hold it up—were first introduced by seal engravers about the beginning of the fourteenth century, to complete their design by filling the space between the flanks of a shield and its enclosing circle. Before the end of the fifteenth century they appear in sculpture and on some of the Garter Stall Plates as an integral part of the Coat of Arms. Soon after this, their use becomes limited (with a very few exceptions) to Peers and Knights of the Garter and the Bath, and in modern times the Knights Grand Cross of all Orders. The historical basis of this limitation is no doubt that only the mediæval owners of great baronial Seals had by usage acquired a prescriptive right to Supporters.

The Badge (q.v.) was a mark of allegiance or ownership, borne alone

16

(without shield, helmet or other frame) by a great lord's retainers on their livery, or used decoratively on the owner's house, tomb or movable goods. The Bear and Ragged Staff of the Earls of Warwick (No. 46) is a well known example. The fashion for Badges came in with private armies in the fifteenth century, during which they were widely used. Under the Tudors, royal Badges alone were numerous. Their subsequent occurrence is rare.

Blazon

A blazon is the description of a Coat of Arms in technical language. A number of principal terms and a conventional order of description had crystallized by the early thirteenth century, when we find them used in Glover's Roll. Their earlier development may to some extent be traced in the descriptions of Arms occurring not infrequently in French chivalric romances.[1] In England down to the fifteenth century all blazon was (apart from some rare Latin examples, cf. Nos. 39, 43) in French. At this stage there were only a few special technical terms, such as the colour names gules and sable, and the names of essentially heraldic things such as fesse, barre, torteaux, verree. When in the second half of that century English blazon came into use, many French terms in more or less Anglicized form were taken over as technical names, and it is at this point that the tendency to make blazon mystifying and unintelligible to the vulgar really begins. It is fair to say that this, like other extravagances, has been more marked in writers of theoretical treatises than in practising Heralds. Much, too, of the complication of terms has been due to the fact that with the passage of time and consequent great increase of the number of coats existing, ever more minute and precise distinctions have had to be made, so that terms of wide extension have been limited in meaning and new names given to new sub-species. In the present century Mr. Oswald Barron, Maltravers Herald Extraordinary, and others have urged a return to primitive simplicity. My aim in these notes has been to give at the head of each a blazon in conventional modern terms. From the eighteenth century onwards, these blazons are where possible in the actual terms of the original Grants. In other cases I have, when in doubt, preferred intelligibility to consistency. In the earlier notes I have, where I could, included also a contemporary blazon of each coat.

[1] Mémoires de la Société Nationale des Antiquaires de France, 5ième série. Tome II, pp. 169-212, Le langage heraldique au XIIIe siècle dans les poêmes d'Adenet le Roi, par M. le Comte de Marsy.

The essential rule of blazon is to begin with the tincture (colour) of the field or background, next to name the principal ordinary or geometrical figure, thirdly any other charges in the field, and fourthly any charges upon the ordinary. Developments of this are dictated mainly by common sense and may be sought out among the numerous examples below.

Heraldic tinctures comprise two metals, Or and Argent, and five colours in general use, Gules, Azure, Sable, Vert, and more rarely Purpure. For aesthetic reasons metal is not normally charged upon metal, nor colour upon colour.

The principal Ordinaries, or geometrical figures, are the Fess, Bar, Gemels, Chevron, Bend, Pale, Cross, Saltire, Chief, Bordure, Quarter, Canton, Pile, Label, Tressure, Dance, Fret, Lozenge, Fusil and Mascle, with which may perhaps be grouped also the Annulet and Billet. The Ordinaries are themselves often varied by the variation of their boundary lines, which, instead of straight, may be Indented, Engrailed, or the like. Repetitions of Bars, Chevrons, Pales, Bends, produce Barry, Chevronny, Paly, Bendy fields. Other variegated fields are those produced by repetitive subdivisions (called by old heralds Gritty), such as Chequy and Vair, or by powdering the surface evenly, with small charges such as Ermine and Flory.

Of the natural charges of Heraldry, the beasts, birds, monsters and inanimate objects, little need here be said. The enrichment of common zoology with fabulous additions and corrections is characteristic of the Middle Ages in general, not only of Heraldry. Heraldry does, however, seem to be responsible for at least one convention of nomenclature. The same beast is in one position (the rampant) a Lion and in another (the passant guardant) a Leopard. This, no doubt, is merely for convenience. Both are very common in Heraldry, and short names for them would therefore be wanted. Most people probably had little or no idea what the difference between a lion and a leopard was. So why not use the two names in this convenient way? There are modern parallels.

A class of charges based on natural or artificial objects but representing them in a conventionalized way, includes among others the Martlet, Fleur de Lys, Quatrefoil, Cinquefoil, Estoile, Escallop, Mullet, Fer de moline and Maunch. Other objects again are drawn naturalistically. In this way Heraldry is a valuable record of obsolete weapons, tools and fashions, and of other archaeological material. Nor does this end with the Middle Ages, for Heraldry gives, for instance, what seems to be the first known drawing of a turkey in the Crest granted in 1550 to William Strickland of Boynton, who commanded one of the ships in Sebastian Cabot's American voyage, when the bird was possibly brought to England for the first time.[1]

Marshalling

Marshalling is the arrangement of two or more coats in one shield to signify union of lordships, marriage, descent, or the holding of office, There are three methods—Impalement (with its variant Dimidiation), Quartering and Superimposition. Impalement means the division of the shield into two halves by a central, vertical (or palewise) line. In impalement proper, each of these two halves holds an entire Coat; but in the primitive method of Dimidiation the Coats are themselves halved so that only the dexter half of one and the sinister half of the other will appear (in No. 18 the sinister coat, being the voided escutcheon of Balliol, but not the dexter, is dimidiated; this use of dimidiation for bordures and similar charges still survives).

The most frequent early use of impalement is on the seals of married ladies, their husbands' Arms generally appearing on the dexter (the more important), and their own paternal Arms on the sinister side (as in No. 61). Where, however, the lady's own family or inheritance excelled in importance those of her husband, her coat would in early times often appear on the dexter side (as for No. 18, Dervorguilla de Balliol).

A second use of impalement is to combine the Arms of an office (e.g. a bishopric, Nos. 51, 66, 71, 88) with those of the holder for the time being, the former appearing on the dexter, the latter on the sinister side. I have seen no example older than the middle of the fourteenth century.

Quartering seems in all the early examples to signify a union of lordships (e.g. in Nos. 28, 41, 50, 52, 53, 61, France and England; No. 43, Percy and Lucy; No. 39, Ireland and Vere; and No. 46), and the superimposed shield was originally used, though but rarely, in a similar way (e.g. Hugh Balliol, under No. 18).

About the end of the fifteenth century, however, when with the passing of the Middle Ages the practical use of Heraldry in war and tournament yielded pride of place to the decorative and commemorative, marshalling began to be used to indicate descent and heirship in blood rather than lordship. The modern practice, which crystallized under the Tudors, is as follows. A husband impales his wife's Arms with his own, unless she be her father's heir or

[1] Information from A. G. B. Russell, Lancaster Herald.

coheir* in blood (that is to say, if she has no brothers), when he displays them on an escutcheon of pretence, superimposed in the centre of his own shield. In the latter case only, the children acquire a right to quarter the Arms of their mother's family (and any quarterings previously acquired in the same way by that family) with their father's. In this way a shield of many quarterings indicates a succession of heiress marriages, so that the bearer represents in blood all the families whose Arms he quarters (Nos. 64, 82). The rule that an unmarried lady shall bear her Arms in a lozenge without Crest (No. 119) dates from 1562.

Use and Authority

The first to use Arms were the great lords and sovereigns, but before the middle of the thirteenth century their use was widespread among knights. By 1410 a non-armigerous gentleman was a rarity needing explanation[1]; and an Act of the Scots Parliament of 1430 implies that every freeholder was expected to possess a seal of his Arms.[2] The view that Arms were 'ensigns of nobility' was already current at this date,[3] though the conflicting theory was likewise held that any man might assume Arms at will.[4] The growth of the former view at the expense of the latter was probably promoted by the practice of admitting to the more important tournaments only noblemen 'of four quarterings',[5] whose claims were examined by the Heralds. The doctrine that Arms were property, so that no man might use those already adopted by another, is implied in a German document of 1286[6] and assumed in an English court of law before 1348.[7] From this it was no great step for the Crown to

[1] Grey and Hastings Controversy, ed. C. G. Young, York Herald, privately printed, 1841, p. 29. 'Johan Lee Escuier del county de Buckingham est gentilhomme d'auncestry & xx. marcz de terre luy sont descendus & n'ad use point de travailler en guerre ne son pier devant luy et pour ce ne prist gard de prendre ses armes'.

[2] The Acts of the Parliaments of Scotland, 1814, Vol. II, p. 19.

[3] A form of Charter given in the formulary of Johann von Geylnhausen, registrar of the Imperial Chancery under the Emperor Charles IV, from 1366 to 1369, refers to Arms as 'nobilitatis insignia' (G. A. Seyler, Geschichte der Heraldik, 1885, p. 342). Richard II of England, by Letters Patent dated 1 July 1389 received Johan de Kyngeston into the estate of gentleman and granted him Arms (Rymer's Foedera, Vol. VII, p. 630).

[4] Bartolo de Sasso Ferrato (d. 1356), printed by Sir Edward Bysshe, In Nicholaum Upton Notae, 1654, p. 6.

[5] Parties inédites de l'œuvre de Sicile heraut, par feu le P. Roland, 1867, p. 98.

[6] Seyler, pp. 811-12.

[7] In the dispute between Nicholas, Lord Burnell, and Robert, Lord Morley, tried by the Constable and Marshal during the siege of Calais.

forbid all bearing of Arms without its authority. In 1417 Henry V addressed Letters Patent to the Sheriffs of three counties declaring that, whereas in recent expeditions abroad many persons had taken to themselves Arms and tunics of Arms called 'Cotearmures' which neither they nor their ancestors had used in time past, no man of whatever rank should henceforth take Arms unless he possessed them by ancestral right or by the grant of some person having authority sufficient thereunto.[1] In the same year Henry V created the new heraldic office of Garter Principal King of Arms of Englishmen;[2] while then or not long after, his brother, Thomas, Duke of Clarence, seems to have issued ordinances in which the right of Kings of Arms to give Arms to persons within their provinces was recognized.[3]

The oldest known King of Arms' Patent is that issued by Sir William Bruges, the first Garter, to the Drapers' Company of London, dated 10 March 1439.[4] While Clarenceux and Norroy Kings of Arms had their provinces of England, South and North of the Trent respectively, in which they might grant Arms, the limits of Garter's jurisdiction were left indefinite when his office was created. Hence ensued much doubt and discussion, not finally concluded until 1673, when it was laid down that all Patents should be issued by the three Kings of Arms jointly and in no case without first obtaining a warrant from the Earl Marshal. In 1680 this was modified so that patents for persons South of Trent should be issued by Garter and Clarenceux and for those North of the Trent by Garter and Norroy. This regulation is still in force. Patents of Arms for Peers, however, are now as they have always been, issued by Garter alone, and those for persons out of the realm by all three Kings of Arms.

Since 1673 all Patents have been recorded in a single series by the College of Arms as a corporation. For earlier Patents we have to rely on more or less full dockets kept by the individual Kings of Arms, on the Patents themselves, and on copies subsequently made from them. Patents vary in purport, some being entirely new grants, some confirmations of a right considered uncertain, and some exemplifications under a Royal Licence authorizing the transfer of Arms from one family to another. The commonest limitation is to the grantee and his descendants, but wider extensions are not infrequent. In the notes the operative words of Patents are where possible cited.

1 Rymer's Foedera, Vol. IX, pp. 257-8.
2 Anstis, Register of the Garter, Vol. II, pp. 322, 327-8.
3 Ib. pp. 323-4.
4 The History of the Worshipful Company of the Drapers of London, 1914, Vol, I, pp. 221-4.

There is evidence that from the fourteenth century at least Kings of Arms were accustomed to make surveys or collections of the Arms borne within their provinces, and many of the anonymous mediæval 'Rolls of Arms' (see pp. 25-31) may well have been their work. In the fifteenth century they had to swear at their creation to do their utmost to have knowledge of all the noble gentlemen within their marches 'and them with theyre issue truely regester and suche arms as they bere'. An early 'Visitation' cited in the notes (No. 94) is that made about 1480 by William Ballard, March King of Arms. The official canon of Visitations, however, begins with the issue of a Royal Commission by Henry VIII on 19 April 1530 for Thomas Benolt, Clarenceux King of Arms. It was addressed to the Sheriffs and other local authorities and directed them that whereas Clarenceux intended 'by waie of noblenes to visite amonge other your armes and conysaunces and to reforme the same yf yt be necessarye and requisite and to reforme all false armorye and armes devysed without auctoritie', they were to give him all assistance in their power. Between this date and 1686, when the last Visitation commission was granted, thirteen were issued for Clarenceux's and seven for Norroy's province, the operation of each ceasing with the life of the individual King of Arms who received it.

The Visitations which followed on these commissions were made county by county, Kings of Arms sometimes deputing Heralds or Pursuivants to visit particular counties for them. Lists of persons understood to claim the title of gentleman and a right to Arms were sent to the county authorities, who summoned them to appear at specified times and places before the visiting Officers of Arms and make good their claims. If these were allowed, their Arms and Pedigrees were entered in the Visitation books. Over a hundred of these are now preserved at the College of Arms, while a few important copies have found their way to other libraries (cf. No. 86). No other country can show a general genealogical survey comparable with that produced in England by the Heralds' Visitations.

The Visitations turned the English Heralds into professional genealogists, and at the present day their time is still largely devoted to the tracing and proving as well as the registration of Pedigrees.

In Ireland Visitations were begun but never extended to more than a small part of the country. In consequence of the resulting lack of ancient record, Ulster King of Arms (whose jurisdiction covers all Ireland) has continued the practice, long since abandoned in England, of confirming Arms on the strength of no more than a century's use.

In Scotland the mediæval theory that the Arms, not merely of each family, but of each individual, should be distinctive, is carried to its logical conclusion, every younger son of an armigerous father having personally to matriculate a differenced form of his paternal coat, before Lyon King of Arms will reckon him armigerous (e.g. No. 122). The existing Lyon Register was instituted in 1672 by an Act of the Scots Parliament amplifying an earlier Act of 1592.

Mediæval Sources

The principle of the present collection has been to require for mediæval Coats contemporary evidence of use, and for modern Coats official registration. The latter having been shortly dealt with in the last section, the nature of the former must now be set out in rather fuller detail.

There are three main sources—Seals, Rolls of Arms, and Monuments. Under the last head, as well as tombs which hardly need discussion, may be classed the superb series of Stall Plates of the Knights of the Garter in Saint George's Chapel, Windsor, the chapel of that Order. The oldest plates (with one exception) date from about 1421, from which time the series continues to the present day. The older Plates were enamelled on gilded metal, the more modern ones painted, until recently, when enamelling was once more adopted. All the Plates down to 1485 were reproduced with notes by Sir W. H. St. John Hope in *The Stall Plates of the Knights of the Garter* 1348-1485 (Westminster, Archibald Constable, 1901).

The Seal, as its owner's personal mark of authentication, provides in most respects the surest evidence we can have of his Arms as he bore them. One thing, however, it omits—the colour. The first appearance of Arms on seals is not in their own right, but as part of the representation of the owner armed and on horseback. They may appear on the shield on his left arm, on the flag upon his lance, and on the trapper of his horse. Before the end of the twelfth century, however, shields of Arms as such begin to appear as seal devices and soon become normal, the greater baronial seals commonly having equestrian figures on the seal and shields of Arms on the counterseal, while the smaller seals have shields of Arms only. Many references are made in the notes to the catalogues of the great collections in the British Museum, at Durham Cathedral, and in the Archives at Paris, as well as to the superb series attached to the Barons' Letter to the Pope in the Public Record Office, and to Laing's great Catalogue of Scottish Seals.

Rolls of Arms is the generic name given to a rather various set of documents. Greenstreet and Russell's 'Reference List of the Rolls of Arms'[1] gives the best account yet printed, but now requires much addition and some correction. The names by which the Rolls are referred to have been given them for convenience by editors and cataloguers. Some of these so called Rolls really are long rolls of vellum (the Camden Roll is 5ft. 3 ins. long and 6¼ins. wide, being made of three skins of vellum sewn together), while others are really books. In one or two cases (e.g. the Fitzwilliam Roll) what were originally Rolls have been cut up and bound in book form. In a large proportion of cases again we possess no originals at all, whether roll or book, but merely copies made by heralds and others in the sixteenth and seventeenth centuries from originals which have since perished or been lost.

Of the originals some are painted with rows of shields in colour, each with the owner's name written above. Others are in blazon only, that is, they consist of written descriptions of the Arms without pictures. A few are both painted and blazoned. A different classification is by contents, and on this principle Rolls may be classed as Occasional, General, Local, Illustrative, and Ordinaries. Occasional Rolls are those which give the Arms of those present on some particular occasion, as for instance the Roll of the Arms of Knights present at the battle of Falkirk in 1298, of those at the Tournament at Dunstable in 1308, of the Parliament of 1523, and the famous Caerlaverock Roll which is a poem giving blazons of the Arms of those who besieged Caerlaverock Castle in July 1300. Most of the Rolls in this class are in blazon.

General Rolls begin usually with the Arms of European rulers, continue with those of Earls and Lords, and finally come down to knights and esquires selected on no evident principle and arranged in no intelligible order. Some, like Glover's Roll, leave out the foreigners; others, like Walford's and the Fitzwilliam, give not only sovereigns but lesser foreign lords. Some of these Rolls are blazoned, some painted.

The third class, that of Local Rolls, is small but important. The chief English example is the great blazoned Roll of 1110 Coats known as the Parliamentary Roll (compiled c. 1310) which covers all England county by county. Still larger is the great Armorial de Gelre, probably the finest heraldic manuscript extant, begun apparently about 1370 by Gelre (the Herald of the Duke of Gelderland), comprising paintings of more than 1800 shields and crests, covering most of western Europe, and arranged by kingdoms and lordships. The English section alone contains 78 shields. The Scottish section

[1] The Genealogist, Vol. V., 1881, pp. 1-18, 94-104, 168-179. *

is a principal authority for early Scottish Heraldry, no mediæval Scottish Rolls of Arms (with one recently discovered exception noted below) being known. This is the oldest Roll whose authorship is known, though it is likely enough that many, in the Occasional and Local classes especially, were the work of Heralds. It is noteworthy that whereas this, like many continental Rolls, gives crests as well as shields, no English Roll does so before the fifteenth century.

The fourth class, of Illustrative Rolls, consists of non-heraldic documents, such as chronicles and cartularies, in the margins of which Arms have been painted by way of illustration. Such are the marginal shields in Matthew Paris' histories and the Warwick Roll.

An Ordinary is a collection of Arms arranged by subject matter, all the coats containing lions, for instance, being grouped together, or all those containing chevrons, so as to facilitate identification. These being essentially practical working books were probably made by heralds. The oldest are Cooke's and Cotgrave's Ordinaries of the reign of Edward III.

The following list indicates the chief editions and manuscripts to which reference is made in the notes.

(I) MATTHEW PARIS SHIELDS

    (1) Illustrative shields painted in the margins of the manuscripts of Matthew Paris' Chronica Majora (Corpus Christi College, Cambridge, MSS. 26 and 16; and Royal MS. 14 C VII in the British Museum), by his own hand or under his direction, between 1217 and 1259; several of these are reproduced in 'The Drawings of Matthew Paris', by M. R. James, Walpole Society, Vol. XIV.

    (2) A leaf of Matthew Paris' 'Additamenta' (British Museum, MS. Cotton, Nero D.I., ff. 170-170b) painted on one side with 35, on the other with 42 shields, being those of a few Sovereigns and of English Earls and Lords. These were edited in the Zeitschrift für Heraldik, Berlin, 1881.

    An index of all the above is given in Matthew Paris' Chronica Majora, Vol. VI, Additamenta, ed. H. R. Luard, 1882, Rolls Series, Appendix I, pp. 469-477.

(II) GLOVER'S ROLL

    Blazoned general Roll of 218 English Coats, c. 1245, ed. 1829 by Sir N. Harris Nicolas as 'A Roll of Arms compiled in the reign of Henry the third' from a transcript made in 1586 by Robert Glover, Somerset Herald. A copy made by Glover in 1585 from another version, and formerly at Wrest Park, is in the writer's possession.

(III) HERALDS' ROLL
(Coll. Arm. MS. B.29, pp. 20-27.) 195 shields, being a fragment of a very finely painted original general Roll of c. 1280.
THE FITZWILLIAM ROLL (Cambridge, Fitzwilliam Museum, MS. 297) is a fifteenth-century painted copy of a more complete original containing 597 shields. A tricked copy of this made in 1590 was edited by Greenstreet as:
PLANCHÉ's ROLL (The Genealogist, New Series, Vols. 3, 4, 5).

(IV) DERING ROLL
Painted Roll of 324 shields, mainly belonging to Kent and Sussex, c. 1280, edited by Greenstreet and Russell from a tricked copy made c. 1607 (Jewitt's Reliquary, Vols. 16, 17, 18).

(V) CAMDEN's ROLL
Original vellum general Roll, c. 1280, with 270 shields painted on the face and 185 of them blazoned on the dorse (British Museum, Cotton Roll, XV. 8), edited by Greenstreet (Journal of the British Archaeological Society, Vol. 38, pp. 309-328).

(VI) WALFORD's ROLL
Lost, blazoned general Roll of 180 Coats, c. 1275, edited by W.S. Walford from a copy made in 1607 (Archaeologia, Vol. 39, pp. 373-388).

(VII) ST. GEORGE's ROLL
Lost painted general Roll of 677 shields, c. 1295, edited by C. S. Percival from two tricked copies made c. 1607. (Archaeologia, Vol. 39, pp. 391-398, 418-446). A sixteenth century copy of a blazoned version of uncertain date (not later than fifteenth century) is in Coll. Arm. MS. M 14, ff. 176-190b and 211b.

(VIII) COLLINS' ROLL
Lost painted general Roll of 598 shields, c. 1295. An edition of this roll by the late Mr. S. M. Collins, F.S.A., based on two sixteenth century

tricked copies and a painted facsimile of c. 1640, unfortunately remains unpublished.

(IX) FALKIRK ROLL

Lost blazoned Roll of 111 English bannerets present at the battle of Falkirk 22 July 1298, edited by Greenstreet from a copy made c. 1606 (Jewitt's Reliquary, Vol. 16). A copy of a slightly longer version made by Glover in 1585 is in the writer's possession.

(X) GALLOWAY ROLL

Lost blazoned Roll of 259 knights present with Edward I in his campaign in Galloway in 1300. An unpublished copy made c. 1550 is in Coll. Arm. MS. M 14, ff. 168-175 (now first noticed).

(XI) CAERLAVEROCK ROLL

A French verse account of English knights banneret and bachelor at the siege of Caerlaverock in July 1300 and their Arms, edited from a copy made in 1587 by Glover, collated with the contemporary copy in the British Museum (Cotton MS. Caligula, A. XVIII, ff. 23b-30b) by Sir Harris Nicolas, 1828, and from the latter only by Thomas Wright, 1864.

(XII) CHARLES' ROLL

Lost painted general Roll, c. 1300. The Society of Antiquaries' MS. 517 is a fifteenth century painted vellum Roll copy, containing 486 Coats, but probably lacking the beginning. C. S. Percival edited this (collating a copy made from it c. 1607 by Nicholas Charles the then owner) in Archaeologia Vol. 39, pp. 389-391, 399-417, 441-446

(XIII) PARLIAMENTARY ROLL

(British Museum MS. Cotton, Caligula A. XVIII, ff. 3-21b.) Original blazoned book of Arms of 1110 English lords and knights banneret and bachelor, c. 1310, arranged for the most part by counties; printed by Sir F. Palgrave with the Parliamentary Writs, 1827, Vol. I, p. 410, and edited by Sir Harris Nicolas as 'A Roll of Arms of the Reign of Edward the Second', 1829, and as 'The Parliamentary Roll of Arms' by Oswald Barron in The Genealogist, New Series, Vols. 11 and 12.

(XIV) BALLIOL ROLL

Lost painted Roll of the Arms of 'Edward Bailoll Roy d'Escoce' and 35 of his nobility. Since Edward Balliol was crowned in September 1332 and only held his kingdom till December, the compilation probably belongs to that interval; known by an unpublished tricked copy made in 1576 (Coll. Arm. MS. Vincent 164, ff. 109b-110b). The only known mediæval Scottish Roll (now first noticed).

(XV) SECOND DUNSTABLE ROLL

Lost blazoned Roll of 135 knights present at a tournament at Dunstable in 1334, edited by C. E. Long from two sixteenth century copies (Collectanea Topographica et Genealogica, Vol. 4).

(XVI) CARLISLE ROLL

Lost blazoned Roll of Arms of 277 knights present with Edward III at Carlisle and in Scotland, July 1334. An unpublished fifteenth century copy illustrated with inexpert paintings is in Fitzwilliam Museum (Cambridge) MS. 324, ff. 105b-128b (now first noticed).

(XVII) COTGRAVE'S ORDINARY

Lost blazoned Ordinary of 556 English Coats, c. 1350; edited, from a copy made in 1562, by Sir Harris Nicolas as 'A Roll of Arms compiled in the reign of Edward III', 1829.

(XVIII) GRIMALDI'S ROLL*

Lost painted and blazoned general Roll of 167 Coats, c. 1350 (or perhaps a fifteenth century compilation from fourteenth century material). John Rylands Library (Manchester) MS. 88 is a fifteenth century painted and blazoned vellum roll copy, edited by Stacey Grimaldi, the then owner, in 1835 (Collectanea Topographica et Genealogica, Vol. 2).

(XIX) ANTIQUARIES' ROLL

(Society of Antiquaries' MS. 136, Part I.) Original painted vellum book of 352 shields of English lords and knights, c. 1355, unpublished.

(XX) ARMORIAL DE GELRE

(Brussels, Bibliothèque Royale, MS. 7516.) A vellum book painted between c. 1370 and c. 1400 by Heynen, Gelre herald of the Duke of

Gelderland, and his successor, with more than 1800 shields and many crests, arranged by kingdoms and lordships and covering most of Western Europe; the greater part edited by Victor Bouton, 7 Vols. 1881, etc.

(XXI) WILLEMENT'S ROLL

Lost painted general Roll of 577 Coats, c. 1395 (preceded by 24 shields of the Founder Knights of the Order of the Garter), edited by Thomas Willement, 1834, as 'A Roll of Arms of the Reign of Richard the Second', from a late fifteenth or early sixteenth century painted vellum copy.

(XXII) BASYNGES' BOOK

(College of Arms MS B. 22, ff. 62-85b.) Original painted vellum book of 407 Coats, c. 1395, sometime the property of Sir John Basynges (d. 1445), unpublished (now first noticed).

(XXIII) 'ROUEN' ROLL

Lost painted general Roll of 177 Coats, c. 1415, wrongly stated by copyists to be of those present at the siege of Rouen 1418; edited by Greenstreet from a sixteenth-century copy (Notes and Queries, 6th series, Vols. 2 & 3).

(XXIV) THOMAS JENYNS' (OR QUEEN MARGARET'S) BOOK

A compilation of 1595 painted and blazoned shields arranged for the most part as an Ordinary. The oldest and best version (British Museum, Add. MS. 40851) seems to have been made for Queen Margaret of Anjou (1445-1482), wife of Henry VI, but incorporates a large proportion of older material, including most of Cotgrave's Ordinary. A much quoted, but now lost, copy belonged to Thomas Jenyns who gave it to Robert Glover, Somerset Herald, who possessed it in 1578 when he made a copy now in the British Museum (MS. Stowe 696). Another sixteenth century copy of this version was the basis of an edition by Greenstreet (The Antiquary, Vols. 1 and 2).

(XXV) RANDLE HOLME'S BOOK

(British Museum, MS. Harl. 2169.) Original book of 1212 tricked coats of the reign of Henry VI, most being of English gentry, but a number royal, foreign and mythical; edited as 'A Fifteenth Century Book of Arms' in the Ancestor, Vols. 3, 4, 5, 7 & 9, and by Joseph Foster (who mistook it for a sixteenth century copy) in 'Two Tudor Books of Arms', De Walden Library, 1904.

(XXVI) BALLARD'S BOOK

(College of Arms MS. M 3.) Original vellum book of about 136 blazoned and 420 painted Coats (excluding later additions by Sir Thomas Wriothesley, Garter), by William Ballard, March King of Arms, c. 1465-1490, and largely belonging to his province of the West of England, Wales and Cornwall; unpublished excepting ff. 35b-42b, which has been edited by Ralph Griffin from a sixteenth century copy made by Glover (Miscellanca Genealogica et Heraldica, 5th series, Vol. 8).

(XXVII) WARWICK ROLL

(College of Arms.) Original vellum chronicle Roll of the Earls of Warwick by John Rous, c. 1480, painted with illustrative shields; a second (the 'Yorkist') version by Rous, then in the Duke of Manchester's possession, was edited by William Courthope, 1859.

(XXVIII) SIR JOHN WRITHE'S BOOK

(College of Arms MS. M 10, ff. 71-123.) Original painted book of 748 Coats (and 76 more in trick), c. 1490, but incorporating earlier fifteenth century matter.

(XXIX) PETER LE NEVE'S BOOK

(British Museum MS. Harl. 6163.) Painted book, c. 1490 and later, of some 2,000 Coats, incorporating a good deal of earlier fifteenth century matter; edited by Joseph Foster in 'Two Tudor Books of Arms', De Walden Library, 1904.

(XXX) PARLIAMENT ROLL OF 1523.

(College of Arms, Box 40, No. 41.) Original painted vellum Roll, by Sir Thomas Wriothesley, Garter, of the Arms of Henry VIII and 61 lords spiritual and temporal present at the Parliament at Blackfriars 15 April 1523; unpublished.

(XXXI) SIR THOMAS WRIOTHESLEY'S ROLL OF PATENTS

(Society of Antiquaries' MS. 443.) Original vellum Roll painted c. 1530 by or for Sir Thomas Wriothesley, Garter, with 420 Coats granted by himself and his predecessors; edited by Mill Stephenson and Ralph Griffin (Archaeologia, Vol. 69, pp. 61-110).

(XXXII) Parliament Roll of 1540
(College of Arms, Box 40, No. 40.) Original painted vellum Roll, by Sir Christopher Barker, Garter, of the Arms of Henry VIII and 68 lords spiritual and temporal present at the Parliament at Westminster, 1540; unpublished.

The Significance of Arms

Contrary to popular belief, most Coats of Arms have no known meaning. Their primary purpose was and is to be distinctive, not significant, and it is certain that many designs have been fixed upon for no better reason than that they happened not to have been used before. But this only makes more interesting these cases in which a definite reason for the adoption of a coat is known or inferred.

A convenient division of 'significant' coats is into Cognate, Canting, and Allusive. By Cognate coats is meant those which are based on others already existing, by reason of kinship, tenure, or allegiance. They arise in three main ways—by Collateral Adoption, Devolution and Differencing. Collateral Adoption belongs to the dawn of Heraldry, and means the simultaneous or nearly simultaneous, adoption of similar coats by a group of men connected with each other by blood or marriage. There is no direct evidence for it, but the arguments of Smith, Ellis, Round, and others are convincing. The classical case is that of the Coats of Say, Vere, Clavering, and Beauchamp of Bedford, all based on the quarterly coat of the great Geoffrey de Mandeville (No. 3), and, in Round's view, all adopted in his lifetime. Other instances may perhaps be found in the groups of chevronny (Nos. 4, 20, 99) and chequy (Nos. 22, 46) coats, and in the group here conjectured to derive from Glanville (No. 5).

Devolution develops the same principle. The reasons for it in particular cases we can only guess, but probably, as Camden puts it, 'Gentlemen' began 'to bear Arms by borrowing from their Lords Arms of whom they held in fee, or to whom they were most devoted'[1] (Nos. 16, 31, 43, 46, 80, 99); though Rye tried to argue that all such borrowings were owing to marriage connections.[2] Later we have the definite evidence of concessions and aliena-

[1] Remains concerning Britain, 1674, p. 277.
[2] Coat Armour used in Norfolk before 1563, Pt. II, 1918, p. 93.

tions, as when in 1442 Humphrey, Earl of Stafford, granted to Robert Whitgreave a shield azure charged with four points of his own coat *Or a chevron gules*.[1]

Differencing resulted from the importance attached in the Middle Ages to the distinctiveness of Arms, extending not only to families but even to the different members of one family. This meant that the paternal coat had to be borne by younger sons with alterations sufficient to distinguish them from the head of their house and from one another, but if possible not so great as to obscure its underlying identity. A treatise has yet to be written on the many methods used for differencing, such as the alteration of colours (No. 108); the addition (Nos. 17, 19, 30, 36, 110), transposition (Nos. 17, 122), or substitution (Nos. 17, 110) of charges; and the addition of labels (Nos. 28, 43, 46, 50), or borders (Nos. 52, 53, 61). It is this system which Scottish Heraldry still continues. In England it gave place about 1500 to the less drastic system of cadency marks, said to have been invented by John Writhe, Garter King of Arms. This consists in the charging on the family coat of minute conventional marks, as the crescent for a second son, or the annulet for a fifth son (See Glossary, under Cadency). In a subsequent generation an annulet would then be charged upon a crescent for the fifth son of a second son, or the fifth son of a second son's descendant in the senior line. But the use even of these marks has now been largely discontinued.

Canting, or punning, coats are highly characteristic of Heraldry at all dates. Certain or probable examples in the present series are sheaves of cummin for Comyn (No. 24), lucies for Lucy (No. 43), sharp mounts for Montagu (No. 34), oxen for Brayboef (No. 132), a castle for Oldcastle (No. 47), staples for Dunstable (No. 55), collets and 'Colette' for Colet (No. 65), moorcock for More (No. 67), a dolphin and eel spears for Fisher (No. 66), cranes for Cranmer (No. 71), roses for Montrose (No. 90), shells for Shelley (No. 119), a spear for Shakespeare (No. 78), wrens for Wren (No. 98), foxes for Fox (No. 113), a swift for Swift (No. 102), and an otter for Coleridge of Ottery St. Mary (No. 124). The exercise of ingenuity coupled with some knowledge of old English and French may well detect hidden puns in still others.

Allusive coats refer, some in obvious, some in cryptic ways, to the achievements, associations or origins of the first bearers. Coats of this type seem (but perhaps only because we lack clues) to be very rare in early Heraldry. The Douglas heart (No. 32), indeed, stands almost alone. Of the many legends

[1] Camden, Remains concerning Britain, 1674, p. 285.

which assign romantic origins to early coats, hardly one stands the test of critical enquiry. Next in time come the Eton lilies in Waynflete's coat (No. 60), and the multiple allusiveness of Wolsey's (No. 63). Augmentations— that is, additions to Arms granted as a special honour by the King himself— may be said to go back to certain grants of Richard II, that to Robert de Vere (No. 39) being one. Such early examples, however, make no allusion to the bearers' deeds or services. This is true of the shield which Henry VIII granted to Edward Seymour (No. 70), though the crest (a phoenix, alluding to Jane Seymour's death in giving birth to Edward VI) is allusive. Elizabeth's Augmentation to Hawkins (No. 74) alludes to his exploits in a general way; but the shield and crest granted to Drake (No. 75) express the nature of his achievement with great accuracy, as does the grant commemorating the exploits of Captain Cook (No. 107). The Churchill (No. 82) and Wellesley (No. 118) Augmentations, like the Seymour, are simply excerpts from the Royal bearings. But those of Nelson (No. 117) and Kitchener (No. 141) refer, if infelicitously, to the nature of their achievements. The ecclesiastical emblems in the Laud (No. 88) and Coleridge (No. 124) coats befit the episcopal grantees. Arkwright's cotton tree (No. 109), Tennyson's laurel wreath (No. 134), Kelvin's thunderbolt (No. 139), and Lister's Aesculapius' rod (No. 140), have obvious appropriateness. The curiously accidental origin of the Sydney Coat (No. 72) would probably, if our knowledge were fuller, be found typical of many.

33

Plate I

I

SIMON DE MONTFORT, EARL OF LEICESTER
Born about 1208, died 1265

SHIELD AND TRAPPER. *Gules a lion rampant queue fourchée argent*

BANNER. *Party per pale indented or and gules*

Design based on a clerestory window in Chartres Cathedral, engraved as the frontispiece of Sir Harris Nicolas' edition of Glover's Roll and in colour, but inaccurately, by N. X. Willemin, Monumens français inédits, Paris, 1825, Pl. 97, and reproduced photographically in C. Bémont's (tr. E. F. Jacob, 1930), Simon de Montfort, p. 224.

Glover's Roll (MS. in the writer's possession), c. 1245, blazons '*Le Comte de Leycester de gules ove un leon blank la cowe furchee et la banner party endente d'or et de gules*'.* Both Coats seem to have belonged to the Montfort family in France, for Earl Simon's father showed the lion on his Seal in 1195 prior to his acquisition of the Earldom of Leicester (Douet d'Arcq, Sceaux de l'Empire, No. 707), while his cousin, Amaury, Earl of Gloucester (d. 1216), sealed with the shield party indented (ibid. No. 10138). The latter was, however, later thought to have been borne by the Earls of Leicester for their Honour of Hinckley, and it is thus given in the Great Coucher Book of the Duchy of Lancaster (Glover's Roll, ed. Nicolas, p. xiv), and (with the spelling 'Henkling' and argent for or) in Harl. MS. 6163, fo. 2b.

Plate I

2

SIR WILLIAM WALLACE
Born about 1272, died 1305

SHIELD AND TRAPPER. (probably) *Gules a lion rampant argent*

SHIELD IN MARGIN. SCOTLAND. *Or a lion rampant within a double treasure flory counterflory gules*

I can find no contemporary authority for the Arms of Sir William Wallace. The Coat, with the addition of a bordure gobony argent and azure, was, however, borne subsequently by the family of Wallace of Elderslie, Co. Renfrew, to which he belonged. (Nisbet's Heraldry, 1712, Vol. I, pp. 285-6). Sir Francis J. Grant, Lyon King of Arms, writes 'Sir William Wallace's Arms are stated to have been, Gules a lion rampant argent. He left no male issue, and after a time apparently an attempt was made to suggest that Elderslie and Craigie were descended of a natural son and hence the border compony. This was not the case, as these

35

families are descended from a previous generation to Sir William'. The pedigree is discussed in The Wallace Papers (Maitland Club, 1841), p. xxx, and in The Book of Wallace (Grampian Club, 1889) by the Rev. C. Rogers. The field is given as azure in Forman's Roll (c. 1562), and such a variation of tincture is not unparalleled in Scottish heraldry, but the weight of authority favours gules. That the Coat antedates Sir William is suggested by the Seal of Sir Richard Wallace, c. 1220 (Laing, Scottish Seals, 1850, No. 839; Birch, British Museum Seals, No. 17035), showing a lion rampant surmounted by a bend. What difference, if any, William bore seems undiscoverable.

For the arms of Scotland see No. 27.

Plate II

3
GEOFFREY DE MANDEVILLE, EARL OF ESSEX
Died 1144

Quarterly or and gules

There is no known contemporary evidence for the use of these Arms by Geoffrey de Mandeville. That he did use them is, however, virtually certain. The argument, worked out by J. H. Round ('Geoffrey de Mandeville', p. 392), rests on the fact that a group of families, including Say, Beauchamp of Bedford, Clavering, Vere, Lacy, and others (Genealogists' Magazine, Vol. 7, p. 469, 'Vere, Lacy and Sackville', by Geoffrey H. White), all connected with one another through Geoffrey de Mandeville and his wife, but not otherwise, are subsequently found bearing different variations of this simple Coat, which was moreover borne by Geoffrey's successors in the Earldom of Essex, cf. Glover's Roll (p. 4), '*Le Comte de Maundeville, esquartele d'or et de gules*'.

Plate II

4
RICHARD DE CLARE ('STRONGBOW'), EARL OF PEMBROKE[*]
Died 1176

Or six chevrons gules

[*] The later Arms of the Clares were, Or three chevrons gules (cf. No. 20), but J. H. Round found in the Public Record Office (Duchy of Lancaster, Grants in boxes, A.157) a Seal of 1141-6 of Strongbow's first cousin, Gilbert de Clare, Earl of Hertford, showing on the shield, which is in profile, the dexter halves of six chevronels (Archaeological Journal, Vol. 51, 1894, pp. 43-8, J. H. Round, 'The Introduction of Armorial Bearings into England'). That chevrons are really meant, though the half-chevrons which appear might be taken for bends,

is proved by the Seal of this Earl's sister, Rohese, Countess of Lincoln (after 1156; Birch, British Museum Seals, No. 13048; attached to Harl. Charter 55. E. 13). A lost Seal of Strongbow's father, Gilbert de Clare, Earl of Pembroke 1138-48, known by old drawings and engravings (Brit. Mus. MSS. Lansdowne 203; Harl. 2044, fo. 94b; Bysshe, In Nicholaum Uptonum Notae, 1654, p. 89), shows a like shield of six chevrons, which appears again on the remarkable counterseal of a man throwing a javelin.

Two Seals of Strongbow himself are known to have existed. One was in 1878 attached to a charter of c. 1172 still at Kilkenny Castle (E. Curtis, Calendar of Ormond Deeds, No. 1), but is now missing (information from the Earl of Ossory). The counterseal, however, was illustrated in the Facsimiles of National Manuscripts of Ireland (1878, Part II, No. lxiii), and (pace the description given there) was clearly identical with his father's counterseal apart from the inscription, which was altered 'SIGILLUM RICARDI FILII COMITIS GISLEBERTI'. This suggests that Strongbow at one time used the six chevrons.

The other Seal was on a charter of c. 1170 still at Chillington (William Salt Society, New Series, Vol. V, p. 212), and is known from a drawing made in 1631 (MS. Harl. 5816, fo. 36b; Journal of the British Archaeological Association, Vol. X, p. 271). This shows an equestrian figure whose shield is charged with three entire chevrons. Unless the drawing is in error (and if the Seal were in poor condition error would be easy) we must suppose that Strongbow was the first of his family to make the change from six to three chevrons.

The Fitzwalters, descending from Strongbow's great-uncle, Robert fitz Richard, bore, Or a fess between two chevrons gules (see No. 99). The Daubeneys of Belvoir, descending from the marriage of William Daubeney 'Brito' with Maud, daughter of Robert fitz Richard, bore, Or two chevrons and a border gules. The Montfichets derived from the marriage of William Montfichet to Margaret, sister of Strongbow's father, their Coat, Gules three chevrons or a label azure.

Plate II

5
RANULPH DE GLANVILLE, CHIEF JUSTICIAR
Died 1190

Or a chief indented azure

No contemporary evidence, but virtual certainty by inference. This Coat, with the addition of *a crozier in bend, or on the azure and gules on the or,* was used by Butley Priory, Suffolk (Coll. Arm. MS. L 10, fo. 67), which Ranulph de Glanville founded. It was borne without alteration by Ralph fitz Ranulph, Lord of Middleham (Glover's Roll, '*Rauf le fitz Randolf, d'or ung cheif endente d'azure*'), grandson of Robert fitz Ralph and his wife Helewise, youngest daughter of Ranulph de Glanville (C. T. Clay, Early Yorkshire Charters, Vol. V, 1936, p. 302); by the Fitz Randalls of Spennithorne, descendants of Ralph fitz Ranulph's younger brother, down to 1517 (Victoria County History, Yorkshire, North Riding, Vol. I, 1914, pp. 258-9); by Sir John de Sandwich (Camden and Dering Rolls), probably brother of Sir Henry de Sandwich, first husband of Joan, daughter and heir of Sir William d'Auberville, grandson of William d'Auberville and his wife Maud, daughter of Ranulph de Glanville; and by Theobald Butler, butler of Ireland (St. George's and Segar's Rolls), great-grandson of Theobald Walter, son of Hervey Walter by Maud, daughter and coheir of Theobald de Valoignes and sister of Bertha, wife of Ranulph de Glanville. It is still borne by Theobald Butler's heir male, the Marquess of Ormonde. The bearing of identical Coats by these three families can be explained only by a common derivation from the notable figure in whom alone their pedigrees converge, Ranulph de Glanville. Differenced versions were borne by Sir William d'Auberville (d. 1245; *a chief indented, two annulets in chief and one in base*; J. R. Planché, Corner of Kent, 1864, p. 291), Sir Ralph de Sandwich (*azure a chief indented or*; Dering Roll), another brother of Sir Henry, and by the Kentish families of Bocton and Goshall (Dering Roll), possibly connected with d'Auberville. Friar Brackley's book of arms, c. 1450 (The Ancestor, No. 10, p. 91) gives *Azure a chief indented or* for 'Mounsire le Glanvyle'.*

Plate II

6

GEOFFREY FITZ-PIERS, EARL OF ESSEX
Died 1213

Quarterly or and gules a border vair

John Charles Brooke, Somerset Herald's, manuscript 'Aspilogia' (Vol. I, p. 12, No. 62) in the College of Arms, has a sketch of a Seal of the Arms, *Quarterly and a border vair*, between two wyverns, with this note—'Geoffrey Fitz-Piers, Earl of Essex . . . ob. . . . 1213. . . .This drawing fm. an impression on paper penes B. Bartlett, f.s.a., Decr 1777, taken fm. the original Matrix fd. at Kenilworth Castle in Co. Warw:'. I cannot trace the present whereabouts of this matrix and have no other direct evidence of this Earl's Arms. That he should have borne this Coat, seems however, probable enough. His first wife (by whom he acquired the Earldom) was Beatrice de Say, great-niece of Geoffrey de Mandeville (No. 3), the supposed first bearer of the Coat, *Quarterly or and gules*. The sons of this marriage, who succeeded to the Earldom, bore this Coat undifferenced (Glover's Roll, '*Le Comte de Maundeville esquartele d'or et de gules*'). But John Fitz Geoffrey, the son of Geoffrey Fitz-Piers' second marriage with Aveline, daughter of Roger de Clare, Earl of Hertford, and widow of William de Munchanesy, bore the Coat here assigned to his father (Glover's Roll, '*Johan le Filz Geffrey esquartele d'or et de gules ove la bordure de veer*'). There may possibly be some connection between this border vair and the escucheons *barry of vair and gules* borne by Sir Warin de Munchanesy. John Rous, however (c. 1480; The Rows or Warwick Roll, ed. W. Court-hope, 1859, arms endorsed on the roll, No. 44), attributes *Vair* to Geoffrey's father, Piers de Ludgarshale.

Plate II

7

EUSTACE DE VESCI
Surety of Magna Carta. Born about 1170, died 1216

Gules a cross paty argent

Matthew Paris shields, MS. Cotton, Nero D.I., fo. 170b, and marginal paintings in his 'Chronica Majora' (Rolls Series, Vols. II, p. 666, & V, p. 410) and 'Historia Anglorum' (Vols. II, p. 187, & III, p. 147). Glover's Roll, in the version edited by Sir Harris Nicolas, blazons his son's Arms, *'Goules a ung croix patonce d'argent'*, this being the sole occurrence in any English Roll of Arms of the otherwise late form *'patonce'* and consequently suspect. Another version of Glover's Roll in the present writer's possession blazons *'Willm. de Vescy de gules od une croiz d'argent furchee'*, a term elsewhere applied to the two-forked or 'moline' cross, but meant here, as a marginal trick shows, for the cross paty.

Plate II

8

WILLIAM THE MARSHAL, EARL OF PEMBROKE AND STRIGUIL, REGENT OF ENGLAND
Died 1219

Party per pale or and vert a lion rampant gules

A shield of these Arms reversed is painted beside the notice of the Marshal's death in Matthew Paris' Chronica Majora (Rolls Series, Vol. III, p. 43; Corpus Christi, Cambridge, MS. 16, fo. 54) and Historia Anglorum (Rolls Series, Vol. II, p. 232; Royal MS. 14, C.7, fo. 104b). Glover's Roll blazons them (for one of his sons) *'Le Conte Mareschall, party d'or et de vert, ung lion rampand goules'*. Two marginal paintings of his eldest son, however, in Matthew Paris' History (Corpus MS. 16, ff. 85, 88b; reproduced, Walpole Society, Vol. XIV, Pl. XII, Nos. 57, 60) show his shield and surcoat charged with hammers and a hammer surmounting his helmet, though above the latter is a painting of the normal 'Scutum Marescalli'. These Arms were transmitted, with the office of Marshal, to the Bigod family (see No. 23). It has been conjectured but not proved that the Coat of the Barons Marshal, Marshals of Ireland— *Gules a bend engrailed* (i.e. *of fusils*) *or*— who were of the same stock, was the original bearing of this family. From this Coat derives probably that of Raleigh. (See No. 80.)

Plate III

9
WILLIAM LONGESPEE, EARL OF SALISBURY
Died 1226

Azure six lions rampant or

On his tomb in Salisbury Cathedral (Stothard, Monumental Effigies of Great Britain, 1832, Pl. 17), given by Matthew Paris (British Museum MS. Cotton, Nero D.I., fo. 170b, and Royal MS., 14 C.7, ff. 111, 148b, Historia Anglorum, Vols. II, 281 and III, 84) and blazoned in Glover's Roll for his son '*Le Conte de Salisbury, d'azur a six lionceulx d'or*'. He was natural son of Henry II, and married Ela, daughter and heir of William Fitz Patrick, Earl of Salisbury. His Arms are identical with those appearing on a remarkable enamel plate formerly in the cathedral and now in the museum at Le Mans (Stothard, Pl.2). This has generally been thought to represent Henry II's father, Geoffrey Plantagenet, Count of Anjou, but according to Sandford (Genealogical History, 1707, p. 114; discussed by J. R. Planché, Journal of the British Archaeological Association, Vol. I, pp. 29-39) it depicts William Fitz-Patrick. According to which view is taken we shall conclude that William Longespee derived his Arms from his grandfather or his father-in-law. Happily Geoffrey H. White (Notes and Queries, Vols. 159, pp. 112-14, and 161, pp. 249-50, and Complete Peerage, Vol. XI Appendix G.) has brought forward arguments which seem conclusive for identifying the enamel as Geoffrey's. It was probably put up on his death in 1150 and fits in perfectly with the account, in his life by John of Marmoutier (Halphen and Poupardin, Chroniques des Comtes d'Anjou et des Seigneurs d'Amboise, 1913, p. 179), of his ceremonial knighting by Henry I of England in 1127, upon his marriage to the latter's daughter Maud. A shield painted with golden lioncels was then hung about his neck (*Clypeus leunculos aureos imaginarios habens collo ejus suspenditur*), and shoes similarly adorned were put on his feet. Geoffrey's younger son, William Fitz Empress (died 1163), bore a single lion (Northants Record Society, Vol. 4, p. 24: Heralds' Commemorative Exhibition 1484-1934, Illustrated Catalogue, 1936, p. 69), as did his grandson King Richard I until 1198.

Plate III

10

FALKES DE BRÉAUTÉ
Died 1226

Gules a cinquefoil argent

A reversed shield of these Arms is painted beside the notice of his death in Matthew Paris' Historia Minor (Rolls Series, Chronica Majora, Vol. III, p. 120; Corpus Christi, Cambridge, MS. 16, fo. 64b; Walpole Society, Vol. XIV, Pl. XI, No. 49). The fifteenth century French 'Armorial de Berry' gives *Argent a cinquefoil gules* for Briauté (information from S. M. Collins, F.S.A.).

1208   1265
SIMON DE MONTFORT.
EARL OF LEICESTER.

1272   1308
SIR WILLIAM WALLACE. GUARDIAN
OF THE REALM OF SCOTLAND.

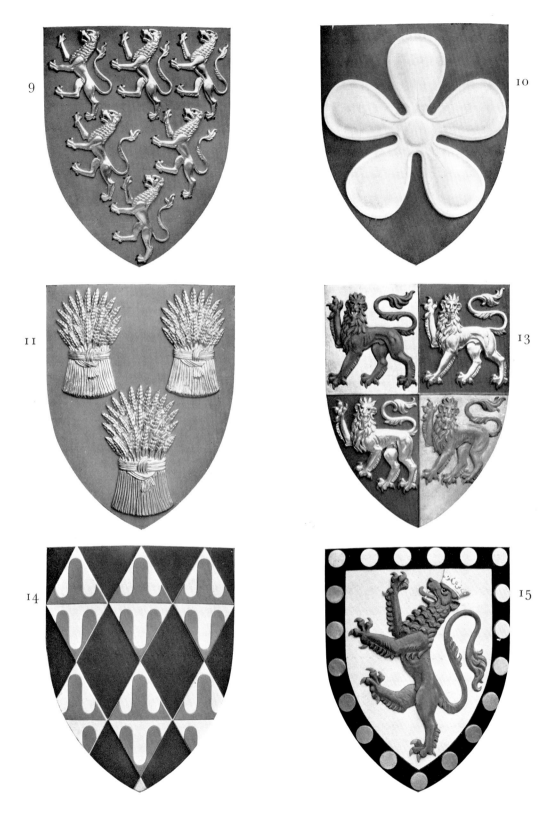

9

10

11

13

14

15

IV

Plate III

11

RANULPH DE BLUNDEVILLE, EARL OF CHESTER
Born about 1172, died 1232

Azure three garbs or

His counterseal (a good example attached to Harl. Charter 52 A. 16, and discussed in the Journal of the British Archaeological Association, Vol. V, pp. 235-252, J. R. Planché, 'On the Seals of the Earls of Chester') shows a shield charged with three garbs. Matthew Paris (Cotton MS. Nero D.I., fo. 170b, etc.) and Glover's Roll supply the tinctures, the latter blazoning, '*Le Conte de Chester, d'azur ove trois garbes d'or*'.

12

ROBERT FITZ WALTER
Died 1235

Or a fess between two chevrons gules

His equestrian Seal attached to Drayton Charter No. 608 (Stopford Sackville Collection, Box 4, Sack 9, at Northampton) shows this Coat on his shield and trapper (information from H. S. Kingsford, Assistant Secretary, Society of Antiquaries), and Matthew Paris (Nero D.I., fo. 170b, and Corpus Christi MS. 16, fo. 95b, Chronica Majora, Vol. III, p. 334) supplies the tinctures. Glover's Roll (c. 1245) blazons for his son, '*Walter le fitz Robert, d'or ung fece entre deux cheverons de goules*'. The Coat is varied from that of Clare (Nos. 4, 20), *Or three chevrons gules*, Robert fitz Walter being grandson of Robert fitz Richard, younger brother of Gilbert fitz Richard of Clare, whose son Gilbert was made Earl of Pembroke. Birch (British Museum Seals, No. 6016) wrongly assigned to this Robert a very fine silver matrix really belonging to his grandson, although John Charles Brooke, Somerset Herald, gave the correct attribution in Archaeologia, Vol. V, 1777, pp. 211-15. Mr. Francis Wormald, F.S.A., however, holds on stylistic grounds that the matrix was originally the grandfather's.

See also No. 99.

Plate III

13

LLEWELLYN AP IORWERTH, PRINCE OF WALES
Died 1240

Quarterly or and gules four leopards counterchanged

No contemporary authority, but the attribution of the coat to Griffith, Llewellyn's son, who died in 1244, by Matthew Paris (Corpus Christi, Cambridge, MS. 16, fo. 169; Walpole Society, Vol. XIV, Pl. XVII), and by several Rolls of Arms to Griffith's son Llewellyn, the last Prince of Wales, appears sufficient warrant. Of these early authorities, however, two (Matthew Paris *supra* cit. and St. George's Roll) give lions passant instead of leopards, but Camden's and Planché's Rolls give leopards, and this form, being that now used for Wales, is here adopted. Yet another thirteenth century roll (Walford's) gives lions rampant, and the arms were borne thus by Owen Glendower (No. 45). Camden's Roll blazons '*Prince de Gales l'escu esquartele d'or et de gules a quatre lepars de l'un en l'autre*', and Walford's '*Llewellin ap Griffith escartelle d'or et de gules iv leons de l'un et l'autre*'.

Plate III

14

HUBERT DE BURGH, EARL OF KENT
Died 1243

Lozengy gules and vair

Seal attached to Brit. Mus. Add. Charter 20, 407; Matthew Paris shields, Cotton MS Nero D.I., fo. 170b; Glover's Roll, '*Le Conte de Kent, masclee de veer et de gules*'. See also No. 112.

Plate III

15

RICHARD, EARL OF CORNWALL
Elected King of the Romans 1257, second son of King John. Born 1209, died 1272

Argent a lion rampant gules crowned or within a bordure sable
bezanty

Glover's Roll blazons '*Le Conte de Cornewail, argent ung lion de goulz coronne or, ung borde de sable besante d'or*'. Matthew Paris has paintings (Cotton MS. Nero D.I., fo. 170b, and Royal MS. 14 C.7, fo. 109b), and there is a fine carving in Westminster Abbey (Historical

Monuments Commission, Westminster Abbey, Pl. 103). J. R. Planché (The Pursuivant of Arms, 1873, p. 171) conjectured that the bezants were peas (poix) allusive to Richard's County of Poitou, but this view has not been generally accepted. Sandford, on the contrary (Genealogical History of the Kings and Queens of England, 1707, p. 95), asserts, without citing evidence, that the crowned lion was taken for Poitou, and the border bezanty for Cornwall. The latter is presumably the basis of the shield, *Sable fifteen bezants or*, used since the late fifteenth century for the Duchy of Cornwall.

Plate IV

16

WALTER DE MERTON, BISHOP OF ROCHESTER
Founder of Merton College, Oxford. Died 1277

Or three chevrons party per pale, the first and third azure and
gules, the second gules and azure

The Arms of Merton College. Woodward (Ecclesiastical Heraldry, 1894, p. 428) with probability derives the Coat from that of Clare, *Or three chevrons gules*.

Plate IV

17

SAINT THOMAS DE CAUNTELO (Cantilupe)
Bishop of Hereford. Died 1282

Gules three leopards' heads reversed jessant de lys or

The original form of this curious Coat seems to be, *Gules three fleurs de lys or*. Glover's Roll blazons for Thomas Cantelo's father '*William de Cantelowe, de goules a trois fleurs delices d'or*'. His Seal (Birch, British Museum Seals, No. 8310) shows the same. Later, however, both the senior and junior branches of the family converted the *fleurs de lys* into *leopards' heads jessant de lys*; cf. for George de Cauntelo of the eldest line (d. 1273), Heralds' College Roll (Coll. Arm. MS. B.29, p. 23; Heralds' Commemorative Exhibition Catalogue, Plate XX); for Nicholas (dead 24 Sept. 1266), brother of Thomas, his Seal of *Three leopards' heads jessant de lys between three cross crosslets* (Birch, No. 8308); for John, another brother, bearing *Azure three leopards' heads jessant de lys or*, the Dering and Camden Rolls; while for his son John the Parliamentary Roll gives '*Sire Johan de Cauntelo de azure a iij flures*

43

de or od testes de lupars yssauns', and for Nicholas' son William (summoned to Parliament 1299), '*Sire William de Cauntelo de goules a une fesse de veer a iij testes de lupars de or'*.

It has been suggested (Complete Peerage, Vol. III, p. 111) that the *leopards' heads* are really *wolves' heads*, in allusion to the name Chante*loup*.

That Thomas Cauntelo bore the Arms in this form seems proved by their adoption as those of his See of Hereford, though his Seal (non-armorial, Birch No. 1605) includes in its design three plain fleurs de lys. That he bore them undifferenced may perhaps indicate that after his nephew's death in 1273 he was the senior male representative of his family.

Plate IV

18

DERVORGUILLA DE BALLIOL
Founder with her husband, John de Balliol, of Balliol College, Oxford, and mother of John Balliol, King of Scotland, 1292-1296. Died 1290

Party per pale; Dexter GALLOWAY, *Azure a lion rampant argent crowned or. Sinister* BALLIOL, *Gules a voided escutcheon* (in modern blazon *an orle*) *argent.*

The impaled shield appears on her Seal (Oxford Balliol Deeds, ed. Rev. H. E. Salter, Oxford Historical Society, 1913, p. 363), and was adopted as the Coat of Balliol College. Dervorguilla's coat is placed on the dexter side, usually occupied by the husband's, probably on account of her great position as coheir of the Lordship of Galloway and transmitter of a claim to the crown of Scotland. Glover's Roll blazons Balliol, '*John de Ballioll, de goules ove ung faux escochon d'argent'*, and for John and Dervorguilla's eldest son, who charged a shield of Galloway in the canton of his father's Coat, '*Hugh son Fitz, autiel, ove ung escochon d'azur ove ung lion rampant d'argent corone d'or en la corniere'*. Hugh Balliol died about 1271 (Northumberland County History, Vol. VI, p. 73).

19

ROBERT BURNELL, BISHOP OF BATH AND WELLS, CHANCELLOR OF ENGLAND
Chief minister of Edward I. Died 1292

Argent a lion rampant sable crowned or

In spite of the absence of direct contemporary evidence that the Bishop used these Arms, it seems certain that he must have done so. He was the sole founder of the fortunes of his

44

family, and made his nephew Philip Burnell (b. 1264, d. 1294) his heir. These Arms are given for Philip Burnell in Segar's Roll, and according to depositions in the Lovel *v.* Morley proceedings (Coll. Arm. MS., Processus in Curia Marescalli, Vol. I, Part 2, p. 161) were on his effigy in the White Friars' church at Oxford. The somewhat different Coats assigned to Philip Burnell in Camden's, St. George's, and Charles' Rolls may relate to an elder Philip, younger brother of the Bishop, or to this Philip prior to his uncle's death.

These Arms were the subject of proceedings in the Court of the Constable and Marshal in 1386, between John, Lord Lovel, heir of the Lords Burnell, and Thomas, Lord Morley (Chancery Miscellanea 6/1, State Papers 9/10, and Coll. Arm. MS. *supra cit.*). For the Burnell Pedigree see Eyton's Antiquities of Shropshire, Vol. VI, p. 134.

20

GILBERT DE CLARE, EARL OF GLOUCESTER AND HERTFORD

'The Red Earl'. Born 1243, died 1295

Or three chevrons gules

Camden's Roll blazons '*Cunte de Gloucestre l'escu d'or od treis cheverons de gules*'. For the early history of this Coat see No. 4.

Plate IV

21

HUMPHREY DE BOHUN, EARL OF HEREFORD AND ESSEX, CONSTABLE OF ENGLAND

Born c. 1249, died 1298

Azure a bend argent, cotised and between six lioncels or

The Falkirk Roll blazons '*Humphrey de Boun Counte de Hereford, Conestable de Engleterre porte d'azur ou ung bende d'argent ou vi leonceaux d'or ou deux cotises d'or*'

Plate IV

22

JOHN DE WARENNE, EARL OF SURREY
Born 1231, died 1304

Chequy or and azure

The Falkirk Roll blazons '*Johan Conte de Warenne cheveteyn de la quarte batayle porte eschekee dor et dasure*'. For his seal attached to the Barons' letter to the Pope see The Ancestor Vol. 6, pp. 186 (Plate), 190. The chequy coat has claims to be the oldest known to heraldry. Ralph was Count of Vermandois from 1116 to 1152. Isabel his sister was married first in 1096 to Robert, Count of Meulan and Earl of Leicester, by whom she had a son Waleran, Count of Meulan and Lord of Worcester; and secondly about 1119 to William de Warenne, Earl of Surrey, from which marriage the subsequent Earls of this house descended. A seal of Count Ralph (Douet d'Arcq, Sceaux de l'Empire, 1863, No. 1010, there dated 1135; but upon what ground does not appear) shows the flag upon his lance apparently chequy. His second Seal of 1146 (Demay, Sceaux de l'Artois et de la Picardie, 1863, No. 38) shows both flag and shield chequy. A seal of Count Waleran, dated between 1136 and 1138 (by Geoffrey H. White, Royal Historical Society, Transactions, 4th Series, Vol. 13, p. 62; engraved, Millin de Grandmaison, Antiquités Nationales, Vol. IV, Art. 44, pp. 17, 19; impression attached to Harl. Charter 45. I. 30), shows shield, trapper and flag chequy. It seems probable that both Waleran's and the Warenne Coat servive from Vermandois (see also Smith Ellis, Antiquities of Heraldry, p. 179). The Coat of the old Earls of Warwick (see No. 46), *Chequy or and azure a chevron ermine*, probably derives from the marriage of Earl Roger (d. 1150) with Gundred, daughter of William de Warenne and Isabel; though this Earl was also first cousin on his father's side of Earl Waleran.

23

ROGER BIGOD, EARL OF NORFOLK, MARSHAL OF ENGLAND
Born 1245, died 1306

Party per pale or and vert a lion rampant gules

The Coat of the Marshals (see No. 8), whose heiress was this Earl's grandmother. His predecessor, though he enjoyed the Marshalcy, kept the old Bigod Coat, *Or a cross gules* (cf. his seal and Glover's and St. George's Rolls). The Falkirk Roll blazons '*Roger Bygot Conte et Mareschal dengleterre porte parti dor et de vert a un leon rampant de goules*'. For his Seal attached to the Barons' letter to the Pope, see The Ancestor, Vol. 6, pp. 192 (Plate), 193-4.

24

JOHN COMYN, CALLED THE RED, LORD OF BADENOCH
Died 1306

Gules three garbs or

Walford's Roll blazons, probably for this John's father, '*John Commin, gules troiz garbes d'or*'. This is possibly a canting coat, the garbs being of cummin.

Plate IV

25

RALPH DE HENGHAM, CHIEF JUSTICE OF THE KING'S BENCH
Died 1309

Argent two chevrons gules between (six) martlets sable

His Seal (Blomfield, History of Norfolk, 1809, Vol. II, pp. 443-4) shows this Coat, but with five martlets and without tinctures; while the Erdeswick Roll, c. 1295, gives it as above, but unnamed. S. M. Collins (editor of this Roll) states that this pattern is otherwise unknown in English mediaeval heraldry, so that it seems safe to assume that the Coat in the Erdeswick Roll is Hengham's. A seal of Sir Andrew de Hengham on a charter of 1294 (Norfolk House Deeds, Box 11) shows *Two chevrons between five birds*, but the Norfolk and Suffolk Roll (Queen's Coll. Oxford MS 158 p. 301) gives for '*An: Hengham*' *Azure two piles ermine*.

Plate VII

26

ANTHONY BEK, BISHOP OF DURHAM
Died 1311

Gules a fer de moline (millrind or cross moline) ermine

The Parliamentary Roll blazons '*Le Evesque Antoyn de Dureem e Patriark de goules a un fer de molyn de ermyne*'. The millrind appears as decoration on the Bishop's Seal (Birch, Brit. Mus. Seals, No. 2452; Hunter Blair, Durham Seals, No. 3125, Pl. 50).

47

Plate V 27
ROBERT BRUCE, KING OF SCOTS
Born 1274, died 1329

SHIELD, COAT AND TRAPPER. SCOTLAND. *Or a lion rampant within a double tressure flory counterflory gules*

CREST. SCOTLAND. *On a mount vert semé of flowers gules a lion sejant gules within a crown and crowned or, holding a sword argent hilt and pomel vert*

SHIELD IN MARGIN. BRUCE. *Or a saltire and chief gules*

The Arms of Scotland appear first on the Great Seal of Alexander II (1214-49; Laing, Scottish Seals, 1850, No. 11; Hunter Blair, Durham Seals, No. 3079). Walford's Roll (c. 1280) blazons '*Le Roy d'Escoce, d'or un lion rampant et un borde florette de gulez*', and the unpublished blazoned version of St. George's Roll (Coll. Arm. MS., M. 14, fo. 176), '*Le Roy d'Escosse porte d'or a ung lyon rampant et un double trace fleurete de gueules*'. The date of this version is, however, doubtful and the closeness of this blazon to that of Nicholas Upton (De Studio Militari, ed. Bysshe, 1654, p. 242), '*Il port d'or ung double trace flourete countre, et ung leon rampant de gewlez*', suggests the fifteenth century. The Crest is taken from the Armorial de Gelre (R. R. Stodart, Scottish Arms, 1881, Vol. I, Pl. A), where it is shown for Robert's son David II (1329-71), with the arms of Bruce displayed in an unusual way on the mantling. The Seal of Robert II (1371-90; Laing, No. 33) shows a lion statant guardant for Crest. Glover's Roll (c. 1245) blazons for Robert's great-grandfather '*Robert de Brus, d'or ung saultoir de goules et ung chief de goules*', and his Seal (Laing, No. 138) shows the same Arms, but Robert's father, Earl of Carrick jure uxoris, sometimes charged the chief with a leopard (Laing, No. 140).

Plate VI 28
EDWARD, PRINCE OF WALES, 'THE BLACK PRINCE'
Born 1330, died 1376

SHIELD, COAT AND TRAPPER. *Quarterly;* 1 *and* 4, FRANCE ANCIENT, *Azure semée of fleurs de lys or.* 2 *and* 3, ENGLAND, *Gules three leopards or*
Over all a label of three points argent

CREST. *A leopard (lion statant) crowned or gorged with a label of three points argent*

SHIELD FOR PEACE. *Sable three ostrich feathers quilled and passing through scrolls argent bearing the words 'Ich Dien'*

From his Seal (Sandford, Genealogical History, p. 125) and his tomb at Canterbury (Stothard, Monumental Effigies of Great Britain, 1817, Plates 85, 86). His actual crest, shield and

VI

1330   1376

EDWARD. PRINCE OF WALES.
THE BLACK PRINCE.

jupon, which still hang above his tomb at Canterbury, show no label (Society of Antiquaries' Heraldic Exhibition Catalogue, 1896, No. 1, Plates I-III). The Arms 'for peace' are mentioned in his Will, where he directs that at his burial two men armed in his Arms and his Helmets shall go before his body, one for war with his Arms quartered, the other for peace with his Badge of ostrich feathers, with four banners of the same, and that he who shall be armed for war shall have an armed man bearing after him a black pennon with ostrich feathers.

The shields for war and peace alternate on the sides of the tomb. The ostrich feather badge is well discussed by Thomas Willement in his Heraldic Notices of Canterbury Cathedral, 1827, pp. 45-9. St. John Hope (Heraldry for Craftsmen and Designers, 1913, p. 166) suggests that it may have alluded to the County of Ostrevant, an appanage of the house of Hainault, and been introduced by Queen Philippa.

For the feathers see further Archaeologia Vol. XXXII, p. 332 and Gentleman's Magazine, 1847, ii. p. 72, and 1851, ii. pp. 527, 620. For the mottoes ICH DIEN and HOUMOUT see Archaeologia, Vol. XXXI, pp. 350-84, XXXII, pp. 69-71 and 332-4, and Notes and Queries, 2nd Series, XI, p. 293. The Ostrevant suggestion was first made by Sir Harris Nicolas.

Plate VII

29

PIERS GAVESTON, EARL OF CORNWALL
Born about 1284, died 1312

Vert six eagles displayed or

Parliamentary Roll—'*Le Counte de Cornewaille, de vert a vi egles de or*'.

Plate VII

30

AYMER DE VALENCE, EARL OF PEMBROKE
Died 1324

Burelly argent and azure an orle of martlets gules

Parliamentary Roll—'*Le Counte de Penbroc, burele de argent e de azure, od les merelos de goules*'. These Arms are superbly rendered on the tomb in Westminster Abbey of this Earl's father, William de Valence, who was third son of Hugh le Brun of Lusignan and Valence, Count of la Marche (by Isabel, widow of King John), of whose Arms, *Burelly argent and azure*, these are a differenced version.

49

Plate VII

31

HUGH LE DESPENSER, LORD LE DESPENSER AND EARL OF WINCHESTER
Born 1261, died 1326

Quarterly argent, and gules fretty or, over all a bend sable

The Parliamentary Roll blazons '*Sire Hue le Despenser, quartile de argent e de goules a une bende de sable les quarters de goules frette de or*'; and the Galloway Roll, '*S. Hugh le Despenser porte quartele dargent et de sable e les quartiers de gueules les frettes dor e en largent ung baston de sable*'.* This Coat appears to be derived from that of Mandeville, *Quarterly or and gules* (see Geoffrey de Mandeville, No. 3), by way either of Beauchamp of Bedford (different members of this family bore, *Quarterly or and gules a bend gules, Quarterly or and gules a bend sable, Quarterly argent and sable*, and, *Gules fretty argent*; Rohese, daughter of Aubrey de Vere and widow of Geoffrey de Mandeville, married secondly Payn de Beauchamp of Bedford), or Lacy (*Quarterly or and gules a bend sable*; John, Constable of Chester, ancestor of this family, married Alice daughter of Alice de Essex, sister of the Countess Rohese above mentioned, cf. Genealogists' Magazine, Vol. 7, pp. 469-72, Geoffrey H. White, 'Vere, Lacy and Sackville'), either because the Despensers were tenants of the Beauchamps of Bedford (J. H. Round, Peerage and Family History, pp. 304, 328), or because they were dispensers to the Constables of Chester (Complete Peerage, Vol. IV, pp. 259-60). The Beauchamp derivation has the merit of suggesting an origin for the *fretty*, as well as the *quarterly* element, in the Coat.

Plate VII

32

SIR JAMES DOUGLAS, LORD OF DOUGLAS
Called the Good. Died 1330

Argent a heart gules, on a chief azure three mullets argent

The Arms of Douglas were originally, *On a chief three mullets* (cf. the seal of Sir William Douglas, 1296, 'The Douglas Book', by Sir William Fraser, 1885, Vol. I, p. 17). The heart was added in allusion to the journey undertaken by the Good Sir James in 1330 in fulfilment of the dying request of King Robert Bruce that he should convey his heart to the Holy Sepulchre at Jerusalem, as an attonement for his failure to perform a vow of pilgrimage thither (Douglas Book, Vol. I, p. 173). Sir James was killed in battle in Spain on his way to Palestine, and both his body and the heart of Bruce were brought back to Scotland. The heart appears on a seal attributed to William, the son (ib. p. 190), and on that of Hugh, the brother (ib. p. 199) of Sir James. Fraser (ib. p. 190) concludes that 'the heart was introduced into the armorial bearings of the Douglas family immediately after the death of the Good Sir James'; but since it appears on the tomb erected to him at St. Bride's by his natural son Archibald about 1390 (ib. p. 181), it seems not unreasonable to suppose that it may have been adopted by Sir James himself on his last journey. The tinctures are supplied from the Arms of William, Earl of Douglas, Sir James's nephew, as given in the Armorial de Gelre.

Plate VII

33
ROGER MORTIMER, EARL OF MARCH
Born 1287, died 1330

Barry, a cheif paly and corners gyronny, or and azure, an escucheon argent

The Parliamentary Roll blazons '*Sire Roger de Mortimer, barre de or e de azure od le chief palee les corners geroune a un escuchon de argent*'. For his father's seal attached to the Barons' Letter to the Pope, see The Ancestor, No. 6, p. 196 (Plate). Oswald Barron, F.S.A., Maltravers Herald Extraordinary, conjectures that this strange coat was originally *Argent a border chequy* (or *gobony*) *or and azure*, deriving from the *chequy or and azure* of Warenne with whom Mortimer was connected. S. M. Collins, F.S.A., however, points out that the use of a very similar Coat by the French house of Pressigny makes this view difficult. Another theory was put forward by Mr. Collins himself in the New England Historical and Genealogical Register, Vol. 99, pp. 271-9. This, however, the writer finds himself unable to accept.

Plate VIII

34
WILLIAM DE MONTAGU, EARL OF SALISBURY
Born 1301, died 1344

Argent three lozenges (or *fusils*) *in fess* (or *a fess engrailed of three points*) *gules*

Second Dunstable Roll—'*Monsr. William de Montagu porte d'argent ove un fece engrele de goules ove trois poynts*'. Planché (Pursuivant of Arms, 1883, p. 80) suggests that there may be an allusion to the name Mont-*aigu*, in the sharp pointed fusils. See also No. 46.

51

Plate VIII

35

SIR JOHN CHANDOS, KNIGHT OF THE GARTER
Died 1370

Argent a pile gules

Froissart (ed. Kervyn de Lettenhove, Vol. 7, p. 196) writes, '*Si estoit la banniere Monseigneur Jehan Camdos: d'argent a un pel aguisiet de gueulles*'.

There is a conflict of evidence, since the Stall Plate at Windsor (St. John Hope, Stall Plates of the Knights of the Order of the Garter, 1901, Plate IV) and Willement's Roll make the field or. Neither of these, however, is a contemporary authority, and they probably erred by attributing to Sir John, who was of a junior branch, the Coat of the senior line of Chandos of Snodhill and Fownhope (cf. correspondence in the Times, 17 and 19 Feb. 1938).

The French armorial of Navarre King of Arms, c. 1370, confirms Froissart, giving '*M. Jehan Chandos, d'argent a ung pail de gueules*' (information from Dr. Paul Adam-Even).

Plate VIII

36

WALTER DE MAUNY, LORD MAUNY
Born about 1310, died 1372

Or three chevrons sable, on the middle chevron a leopard or

This Coat is given and was perhaps used variously. The Antiquaries' Roll gives for '*Mons de Mauney*', *Or three chevrons sable*, without the leopard, as does the Carlisle Roll for '*Mons. Terri de Mawny*', and this was perhaps the undifferenced coat of the house. In the Second Dunstable Roll '*Monsr. Wauter de Manny porte d'or ove trois cheverons de sable ove un leopard d'or en le cheveron*', leaving us to guess which chevron is so charged. In Cotgrave's Ordinary this doubt is resolved, but the leopard becomes a lion passant, '*Monsire Walter de Mauney port d'or a trois cheverons de sable en point en milieu cheveron une lyon passant d'or*'. The Carlisle Roll keeps the leopard but places him on the upper chevron, '*Mons. Wat' de Mawne port d'or ove trois cheverouns de sable un leupert d'or en chief en chiveroun*'. Thomas Jenyns' book (Add. MS. 40851, p. 59) makes him a lion and places him contradictorily on the middle of *two* chevrons, '*Mons. Waultier Mauny port d'or deux cheverons de sable et un lion en point du cheveron milue*'. The painting shows him on the upper.

S. M. Collins, F.S.A., notes the following entries in continental armorials: Roll of the tournament at Compiegne, c. 1270, Jehan de Mauny, *Sable three chevrons argent*; Gelre's Roll, c. 1370. Wouter van Many, *Or three chevrons sable*; Navarre's Roll, c. 1370, Gautier de Maugny, the same.

Plate VIII

37

JOHN WYCLIFFE

Died 1384

Argent a chevron sable between three cross crosslets gules

Herbert B. Workman ('John Wyclif', Oxford, 1926, Vol. I, p. 41) adduces convincing evidence for the view that Wycliffe was second but eldest surviving son of Roger Wycliffe of Wycliffe, Co. York, on whose tomb these Arms are carved (Whitaker, History of Richmondshire, 1823, Vol. I, p. 198). Grimaldi's Roll blazons, '*Robert Wyclif port d'argent ove une cheveron et trois croiseletz de goules*'.

Plate VIII

38

MICHAEL DE LA POLE, EARL OF SUFFOLK

Born 1330, died 1388

Azure a fess between three leopards' faces or

Willement's Roll, No. 130; Birch, British Museum Seals, No. 12755, attached to Cotton Charter xxviii, 85 (see Surtees' Durham, Vol. I, Seals, Pl. 9, No. 18, for a Seal of his father).

Plate VIII

39

ROBERT DE VERE, EARL OF OXFORD AND DUKE OF IRELAND

Born 1362, died 1392

Quarterly, 1 *and* 4 St. Edmund, *or* Ireland. *Azure three crowns or and a border argent;* 2 *and* 3 Vere. *Quarterly gules and or a mullet argent*

By Letters Patent dated 3 Jan. 1386 (Cal. Patent Rolls, 1385-9, p. 78) Richard II authorized Robert de Vere to quarter the Coat here given in the first quarter, '*arma de azuro cum tribus coronis aureis et una circumferentia vel bordura de argento*', with his Arms of Vere so long as he should hold the lordship of Ireland. The coat '*Azure three crowns or*' is that attributed to St. Edmund, which may have been assigned by the King to his favourite on the same

53

principle as his own assumption of the coat of St. Edward. There are some (but not, I think, conclusive) grounds for thinking that the same coat, perhaps in consequence of this grant, came to be looked upon as that of Ireland (Gentleman's Magazine, 1 June 1845, Vol. 115, pp. 603-7, 'Were three crowns the ancient Arms of Ireland?'; and Journal of the Archaeological Institute, Vol. IX, p. 23, J. G. Nichols, 'The Descent of the Earldom of Oxford'). An encaustic tile found in Essex shows the Arms thus quartered (Gentleman's Magazine, 1818, Vol. 88, p. 305).

The Coat of Vere (Glover's Roll blazons '*Le Comte d'Oxenford esquartele d'or et de gules ove une estoille d'argent en le quartier devant*') is one of the group deriving from Geoffrey de Mandeville (see Nos. 3 and 31), whose wife Rohese was sister of Aubrey de Vere, first Earl of Oxford.

40
SIR JOHN HAWKWOOD
Died 1394

Argent on a chevron sable three escallops of the field

Willement's Roll, No. 152; and see E. Chester Waters, 'The Chesters of Chicheley', Vol. I, p. 300. S. M. Collins, F.S.A., notes these arms for James Hawkwood in Gelre's Armorial, c. 1370.

Plate IX

41
JOHN OF GAUNT, DUKE OF LANCASTER
Born 1340, died 1399

Quarterly; 1 *and* 4, FRANCE ANCIENT, *Azure semée of fleurs de lys or.*
2 *and* 3, ENGLAND, *Gules three leopards or*

Over all a label of three points ermine

This is the Coat borne by him as Earl of Richmond, *Ermine* being the Coat of the Dukes of Brittany who held that Earldom before him. It appears on more than one of his seals, (Sandford, Genealogical History, p. 249). Thomas Jenyns' Book (Add. 40851, p. 16), blazons '*John Duc de Lancastre fitz au Roy lez armes de France et d'Engletere a labelles d'ermyn*'

54

As King of Castile he impaled this coat with the quartered Arms of Castile and Leon, and after the surrender of that Kingdom, impaled the same with the Arms of his first wife Blanche of Lancaster; or alternatively, for his Duchy of Lancaster, bore France and England quarterly with *a label of France (Azure with nine fleurs de lys or)*, as appears from a shield which hung over his tomb in Old St. Paul's (Edmund Bolton, Elements of Armories, 1610, p. 69). This *label of France* was first adopted by Edmund, Earl of Lancaster, son of King Henry III, probably upon his marriage in 1276 with Blanche, daughter of Robert, Count of Artois, son of King Louis VIII of France.

Plate IX

42

GEOFFREY CHAUCER*
Born about 1340, died 1400

Party per pale argent and gules a bend counterchanged

MS. Harl. 2169 (The Ancestor, No. 4, p. 250; Foster, Two Tudor Books of Arms, p. 32), a collection of Henry VI's reign, gives this Coat for 'Jafferey Chauserys, Oxynford chyre', at fo. 27, but at fo. 30 (Ancestor, No. 5, p. 178; Foster, p. 36) assigns to him, *Argent a chief gules and lion rampant or over all*. This however, is the Coat of Burghersh, which was adopted by Thomas Chaucer, the poet's son, on his marriage with Maud, daughter of Sir John Burghersh (but cf. Complete Peerage, Vol. VII, p. 194). It occurs at Ewelme, Oxfordshire, on the tomb of Thomas Chaucer's daughter Alice, Duchess of Suffolk.

Plate IX

43

SIR HENRY PERCY, 'HOTSPUR', KNIGHT OF THE GARTER
Born 1364, died 1403

Or a lion rampant azure and label of three points gules

Willement's Roll, No. 81, gives his Arms thus. But a Seal engraved in Archaeologia Aeliana, New Series, Vol. IV, p. 183, shows that upon the death of his stepmother Maud Lucy he added a quartering for Lucy, *Gules three lucies argent* (the whole still differenced by a label), in accordance with the settlement (ib. pp. 174-5; Feet of Fincs 289/54/109; I.P.M. 22 Ric. II, No. 38) whereby it was agreed that if Maud should die without issue her castle and honour of Cockermouth should remain to Hotspur on condition that he and his heirs male should quarter with their paternal Arms '*quae sunt de auro cum uno leone de azuro rampante*', those of Lucy '*quae de gouliis cum tribus lucys argenteis consistunt*'. That Hotspur's father, the Earl of Northumberland, though not obliged to do so by this settlement, likewise assumed the Lucy quartering, is proved by Willement's Roll (No. 39) and by his Seal (Surtees, History of Durham, Vol. I, Seals, Pl. 8, No. 1). The lion coat of Percy (Parliamentary Roll, '*De or a un lion rampaund de azure*') seems to have been adopted by Henry, first Lord Percy, upon his marriage about 1299 to Eleanor, daughter of John Fitzalan, Earl of Arundel, from the bearing of the Earls of Arundel (first of the D'Aubigny, then of the Fitzalan family), *Gules a lion rampant or*. The previous Percy Coat, *Azure five fusils in fess or* (Glover's Roll, '*Henry de Percy d'azur a la fesse engrele d'or*') has without much probability been considered a pun on the notion of piercing (Archaeologia Aeliana, N.S. Vol. IV, p. 164).

Plate IX

44
WILLIAM OF WYKEHAM, BISHOP OF WINCHESTER
Born 1324, died 1404

Argent two chevrons sable between three roses gules barbed and seeded proper

On his tomb at Winchester, and his seal (Herald and Genealogist, Vol. V, p. 226), and used by his foundation New College, Oxford. Charles Wykeham Martin, F.S.A. (Topographer and Genealogist, Vol. 3, pp. 49-74, 'Was William of Wykeham of the Family of Swalcliffe?'; and Herald and Genealogist, Vol. V, pp. 225-45, 'Who was William of Wykeham?'), argued that he was of kin to the Wykehams of Swalcliffe, Oxfordshire, and that they at one time bore this Coat. Basynge's Book (College of Arms MS., B.22, fo. 85b) gives for 'Wikeam', *Gules two chevrons or*.

Plate X

45
OWEN GLENDOWER
Born about 1359, died about 1416

SHIELD, COAT AND TRAPPER. *Quarterly or and gules four lions rampant counterchanged*

CREST. *A dragon (or wyvern) gules*

The design is based on the only known impression, in Paris, of Owen's remarkable Great Seal as Prince of Wales (Douet d'Arcq, Sceaux de l'Empire, Nos. 10135-6; engraved

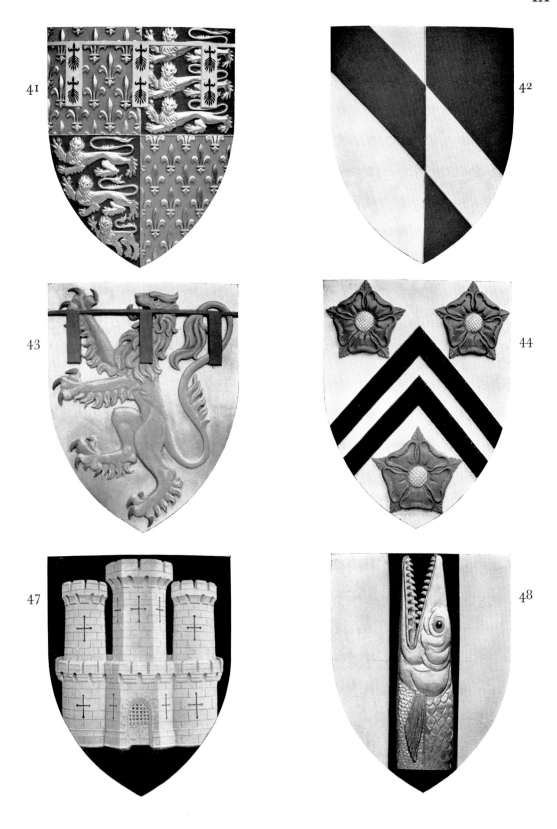

41

42

43

44

47

48

X

45

1359

1416

OWEN GLENDOWER.
PRINCE OF WALES.

in Archaeologia, Vol. 25, p. 616; reproduced photographically as the frontispiece of T. Matthews' 'Welsh Records in Paris', Carmarthen, 1910). The tinctures of the Arms are assumed to be those of the more usual Coat of the Princes of Wales (see No. 13). The dragon is made *gules*, as generally from Tudor times, but might perhaps be *or*, since Adam of Usk (ed. Maunde Thompson, p. 71) states that Owen in 1401 used a standard of a golden dragon on a white field. The British dragon is a preheraldic national ensign. Nennius (Historia Britonum, ed. Joseph Stevenson, English Historical Society, 1838, p. 83) in the eighth century seems to allude to it. Wace in 1155 (Roman de Brut, ed. le Roux de Lincy, 1838, l. 9521) says that King Arthur's helm *'en som ot portrait un dragon'*. The English adopted it, for it appears as Harold's standard on the Bayeux tapestry, and was used by Henry III (J.R. Planché, The Pursuivant of Arms, 1859, p. 97) and as his crest by Thomas Earl of Lancaster (Seal attached to the Baron's letter to the Pope, 1301, The Ancestor, Vol. VI, pp. 191-2; a later one attached to Cotton Charter, xvi, 7, Birch, British Museum Seals, No. 6331). See also Hearne's Curious Discourses, 1775, Vol. I, p. 114.

Plate XI

46

RICHARD NEVILLE, EARL OF WARWICK AND SALISBURY
'THE KING MAKER'

Born 1428, died 1471

SHIELD, OF NEVILLE. *Gules a saltire argent and label gobony argent and azure*

CREST, OF BEAUCHAMP. *Out of a coronet gules a swan's head argent beak gules*

TRAPPER. *Front: Quarterly,* 1 *and* 4, MONTHERMER, *Or an eagle displayed vert.* 2 *and* 3, MONTAGU, *Argent three fusils in fess gules. Back. Quarterly,* 1 *and* 4. *Quarterly, i and iv,* BEAUCHAMP, *Gules a fess between six cross crosslets or; ii and iii,* WARWICK, *Chequy or and azure a chevron ermine.* 2 *and* 3, *Quarterly, i and iv,* CLARE, *Or three chevrons gules; ii and iii,* DESPENSER, *Quarterly argent, and gules fretty or, over all a bend sable*

BADGES. (1) FOR WARWICK. *A bear argent, muzzled and chained gules, supporting a ragged staff argent.* (2) probably FOR NEVILLE. *A bull couchant argent horned or*

The equestrian figure is based on a fine equestrian Seal (see The Ancestor, No. 4, pp. 143-7, and No. 5, pp. 195-200, 'The Arms of the King-Maker', by J. Horace Round, illustrated), from which the unusual marshalling of the Quarterings is taken without alteration. Another (heraldic) marshals them differently—1 and 4, Clare quartering Despenser; 2 and 3 Montagu quartering Monthermer. And yet another substitutes Neville for Montagu and Monthermer in the third quarter. The whole shows well how quartered shields in their origin represented unions of lordships, not, as later, heirships in blood. The original coat of the Nevilles, *Gules a saltire argent* (the seal of their ancestor Robert fitz Maldred, d. 1242-8, bears the saltire; cf. Durham Seals, No. 1242), was differenced with the *label gobony* by Richard Neville, Earl of Salisbury (Hope, Stall Plates, Pl. LV), eldest son of the second marriage of Ralph Neville, Earl of Westmorland, with Joan Beaufort, legitimated daughter of John of Gaunt, who no doubt based his difference on the gobony border of the Beauforts (see No. 52). This Richard married in 1424 Alice, daughter and heiress of Thomas Montagu, Earl of Salisbury, whose grandfather (son of No. 34) had married the Monthermer heiress. Their son, the King Maker, married the daughter and eventual heiress of Richard Beauchamp, Earl of Warwick (who quartered the Arms of the old Earls of Warwick with that of his Beauchamp ancestors who had acquired that Earldom by marriage), by Isabel, daughter of Thomas le Despenscer, Earl of Gloucester, who bore Clare (as the greater Coat and belonging to his Earldom) in the first quarter, and Despenser in the second (Sandford, Genealogical History, 1707, p. 379). The Parliamentary Roll blazons '*Sire Randolf de Nevyle de goules a un sautour de argent*', '*Sire Rauf de Monhermer de or a un egle de vert*', and '*Le Counte de Warwik de goules crusule de or a une fesse de or*'; and Glover's Roll gives the old Coat of Warwick, '*Le Conte de Warrewik chequy d'or et d'azure a ung cheveron d'ermyn*'.

The Beauchamp Crest is well shown on the Garter Stall Plate of Thomas, Earl of Warwick (d. 1401; Hope, Pl. XLI), with mantling Argent and gules. The mantling on the Stall Plate of Richard Neville, Earl of Salisbury (Hope, Pl. LV) is Sable and ermine.

The bear and the ragged staff were originally separate Badges. Both occur repeatedly on the tomb of Richard Beauchamp, Earl of Warwick (d. 1439). Dugdale (Antiquities of Warwickshire, ed. 1765, p. 292) quotes an account of painting for him 'CCCC Pencels bete with the Raggidde staffe of silver'. The Rous or Warwick Roll in the College of Arms (Heralds' Commemorative Exhibition Catalogue, No. 39) shows the bear white with red muzzle and chain, and (beneath the King Maker's feet) the White Bull with golden horns (probably a Neville Badge, since the Lords Latimer and Abergavenny used similar Badges), together with the Monthermer eagle (Burlington Fine Arts Club, Exhibition of British Heraldic Art, Catalogue, Pl. IX). The Bull (which was also a Neville crest) is probably for Bulmer. Geoffrey de Neville married Emma, daughter of Bertram de Bulmer in 1176. From their daughter Isabel, wife of Robert FitzMaldred, the Kingmaker was ninth in descent.

XI

46

1428   1471

RICHARD NEVILLE, EARL OF WARWICK
AND SALISBURY...THE KING MAKER.

Plate IX

47

SIR JOHN OLDCASTLE, LORD COBHAM
Born about 1360, died 1417

Sable a castle triple towered argent

Thus painted in a contemporary armorial (College of Arms MS. B.23, fo. 64b), but there is a conflict of evidence as to the tinctures, the so-called Rouen Roll making the castle sable on argent. The Oldcastle Coat is there and in the Canterbury Cloisters (*Archaeologia*, Vol. 66, p. 515) shown quartered in the 2nd and 3rd with Cobham in the 1st and 4th, Sir John having married the Cobham heiress in 1408 and probably in consequence been summoned to Parliament as a Baron.

College of Arms MS. L.1 (c. 1530) blazons '*Holdcastle beryth silver a castel sable wyndowed and ported of the feld a chayne in fece over the gate gold*'.

Plate IX

48

SIR WILLIAM GASCOIGNE, CHIEF JUSTICE
Born about 1350, died 1419

Argent on a pale sable a lucy's (or conger's) head couped or

On his tomb at Harewood, Yorkshire.

Thomas Jenyns' Book (Add. 40851, p. 100) blazons '*Mons. William Gascoyne port d'argent a une pale de sable ove la teste dune luce dargent en la pale*'. But later writers (e.g. Guillim's Heraldry, ed. 1724, p. 238) make the head a conger's; and even in Jenyns' Book the picture shows a creature of a savage aspect perhaps unusual in the lucy of heraldry.

Plate XII

49

RICHARD WHITTINGTON, MAYOR OF LONDON
Died 1423

Gules a fess chequy or and azure, in dexter chief an annulet or

These Arms (impaling Fitzwarin) were on his tomb at St. Michael's Royal before the fire (drawing in Harl. MS. 1096, fo. 112). He was of the family of Whittington of Pauntley, Co. Gloucester (*vide* Samuel Lysons, 'Model Merchant of the Middle Ages', 1860). This Coat is given in Harl. MS. 2169, fo. 29 (temp. Henry VI; The Ancestor, No. 5, p. 177; Foster, Two Tudor Books of Arms, p. 35) for 'John Wetyngton, Worcester chyre', which makes it clear that the annulet is not, as Lysons thought, a mark of cadency (this would be an anachronism), but an integral part of the coat—perhaps an old difference.

Plate XII

50
JOHN, DUKE OF BEDFORD
Born 1389, died 1435. Third son of King Henry IV

Quarterly, 1 *and* 4, FRANCE MODERN. *Azure three fleurs de lys or*
2 *and* 3, ENGLAND. *Gules three leopards or*
Over all a label of five points, the first two ermine, the last three azure charged
each with three fleurs de lys or

Shown thus on his Garter Stall Plate at Windsor (St. John Hope, Pl. XLIV). His Crest, the royal leopard crowned or, is gorged with a label as in the shield. The Ermine is derived from John of Gaunt, the fleurs de lys from Henry, Earl of Lancaster.

Plate XII

51
HENRY CHICHELEY, ARCHBISHOP OF CANTERBURY
Born about 1362, died 1443

Party per pale. *Dexter.* THE SEE OF CANTERBURY.* *Azure an archiepiscopal*
staff or surmounted by a pall argent fringed or and charged
with three crosses formy sable.
Sinister. CHICHELEY. *Or a chevron between three cinquefoils*
pierced gules

Canterbury Cathedral, Chicheley Porch (Archaeologia, Vol. 71, p. 129 and Pl. VII). Chicheley's Arms have been adopted by his foundation, All Souls College, Oxford.

Plate XII

52
HENRY BEAUFORT, CARDINAL OF ST. EUSEBIUS,
BISHOP OF WINCHESTER
Died 1447

Quarterly, 1 *and* 4, FRANCE MODERN. *Azure three fleurs de lys or*
2 *and* 3, ENGLAND. *Gules three leopards or*
All within a border gobony argent and azure

His tomb in Winchester Cathedral; carving in Southwark Cathedral (Historical Monuments Commission, London, Vol. V, Pl. 112); MS. Harl. 2169, fo. 12 (The Ancestor, No. 4,

p. 225; Foster, Two Tudor Books of Arms, p. 14); windows at Queen's College and Merton College, Oxford, and St. Cross, Winchester (Sandford, Genealogical History, 1707, p. 260). The Beauforts, natural children of John of Gaunt by Katherine Swinford, all adopted borders gobony for difference, but not apparently till after their legitimation in 1397 (Sandford, p. 322); 'Which kind of Border', writes Sandford, 'I have cleared from the Aspersion of Bastardy, in my Marginal Annotations on the Seventh Chapter (last mention'd) of this Fourth Book; where I prove, that not only Humphrey, Duke of Gloucester, Nephew to this John [Beaufort], but also Philip of France, Duke of Burgundy, did (as they were the youngest sons of their Fathers) bear a Border Gobony'; and he further remarks (p. 315) on 'the Ingratitude of those of this last Age [that of Charles II], to the Memory of these Two Illustrious Princes, who have converted the Border Gobony to no other use than the Distinguishing of their spurious and illegitimate Issue, from those lawfully begotten; of which, in these later times, there are too many instances'. The arms born by John Beaufort before legitimation (Coll. Arm. MS. B.22), *Party per pale argent and azure a bend of Lancaster* (i.e. *Gules charged with three leopards or and a label of three points azure each charged with three fleurs de lys or*) are really of a type associated with bastardy. Henry Beaufort seems to have borne before legitimation *Party per pale argent and azure on a chevron gules three leopards or*, which is given for 'The Byschope of Lyncollne' (as he was 1398-1404) in Randle Holme's book (Ancestor No. 7, 199: Foster, Two Tudor Books of Arms, p. 64).

53
HUMPHREY, DUKE OF GLOUCESTER
Born 1391, died 1447. Fourth son of King Henry IV

Quarterly, 1 *and* 4, France modern. *Azure three fleurs de lys or*
2 *and* 3, England. *Gules three leopards or*
All within a border argent

Thus shown on his tomb at Saint Albans (Sandford, Genealogical History, pp. 315, 318). But we learn from Nicholas Upton (De Militari Officio, ed. Bysshe, 1654, p. 238) that he had previously borne the border gobony argent and azure: '*Il port les Armes de Fraunce et d'Engleterre quartelez ovesque ung bordure gobone d'argent et d'asor*'.

Plate XII

54
JOHN TALBOT, EARL OF SHREWSBURY
Born 1390, died 1450

Quarterly, 1 *and* 4, Talbot. *Gules a lion rampant and border engrailed or*
2 *and* 3, Furnival. *Argent a bend between six martlets gules*

Sir John Talbot was summoned to Parliament as Lord Furnival from 1409 following his marriage with the Furnival heiress. His Arms are shown thus on a Seal (illustrated by Hope), but later, succeeding in 1421 to the Baronies of Talbot and Strange of Blackmere, and being in 1442 created Earl of Shrewsbury, he used a shield of four different quarters as his Garter Stall Plate shows (St. John Hope, Pl. LI); 1, probably for the Earldom of Shrewsbury. *Azure a lion rampant and border or.* 2, Talbot, as above. 3. Strange. *Argent two lions passant gules.* 4, Furnival, as above. A shield of four different quarters was at this date still rare, and like most or all early quarterings stands for a union of lordships rather than of blood. The Parliamentary Roll blazons '*Sire Gilberd Talebot, de goules a un lion rampand de or od la bordure endente de or*', and '*Sire Thomas de Fornival de argent a une bende e vj mereloz de goules*'.

Plate XII

55
JOHN DUNSTABLE*
Died 1453. Musician and mathematician

(probably) *Sable a chevron ermine between three staples argent*

John Dunstable the musician was buried in St. Stephen's, Walbrook, London, but a Hertford-shire connection is suggested by the fact that an epitaph on him was written by John Whet-hamstead, Abbot of St. Albans (Fuller's Worthies, 1662, Bedfordshire, p. 116; Weaver, Funerall Monuments, p. 577). In Grove's Dictionary of Music and Musicians (ed. 1927, Vol. II, p. 111) it is suggested that he may have been the John Dunstable, to whom, with Margaret his wife and others, the manor of Bradfield in Cottered, Co. Hertford, was granted by Richard Whaplode, Vicar of Sandon and Steeple Morden, and others, on the 16th of March 1449. But he in turn must probably be the same 'John Dunstaple, armiger', who in 1441-2 was plaintiff in a suit touching lands in Bassingbourne, Steeple Morden and Litlington. These places are in Cambridgeshire, and it is suggested that the musician is the 'John Dunstable of Kambregishere' to whom the above Arms are assigned in a fifteenth century Armorial in the College of Arms (M.10, fo. 113).

Plate XIII

56
JOHN TIPTOFT, EARL OF WORCESTER
Born about 1427, died 1470

Quarterly, 1 *and* 4, TIPTOFT. *Argent a saltire engrailed gules*
2 *and* 3, POWIS. *Or a lion rampant gules*

So shown on his Garter Stall Plate (St. John Hope, Pl. LXVI). The Camden Roll blazons '*Robert Typotot l'escu d'argent a un sautour engrasle de gules*'; and the Parliamentary Roll, '*Ly Sire de la Pole de or a un lioun de goules*'. The Lord of Powis was called 'de la Pole' from his residence at Welsh Pool, Co. Montgomery. This Earl's mother was coheir of Edward Charleton, Lord of Powis, whose great-grandfather had married the heiress of Powis.

Plate XIII

57

SIR THOMAS MALORY

Born about 1410, died 1471. Author of Morte d'Arthur

Quarterly, 1 *and* 4, REVEL. *Ermine a chevron gules and border engrailed sable*
2 *and* 3, MALORY. *Or three lions passant sable*

For the identification of the author of Morte d'Arthur with Sir Thomas Malory of Newbold
Revel and Monks Kirby, Warwickshire, see 'History of Parliament 1439-1509, Biographies'
(H.M. Stationery Office, 1936), p. 568. Harl. MS. 6163, fo. 56b (Foster, Two Tudor
Books of Arms, p. 216) gives the Coat quartered as above for 'Mal Ierre', and Dugdale's
Warwickshire (1730 edn., Vol. I, p. 83) engraves separate shields of Revel and Malory
from 'the parlour windows' at Newbold Revel. John Malory of Winwick, Northamptonshire,
married a Revel coheiress in the time of Edward III. Cotgrave's Roll blazons '*Monsr. John
Rivell port d'or le chief [sic] endente de sable une cheveron de gules*'; that 'chief' is an error for
border is shown by the tricked version (Cooke's Ordinary) in Coll. Arm. MS. Vincent 164,
fo. 93b. The Parliamentary Roll blazons '*Sire Peres Maloure, de or a iij lupars* [not *lions*]
passaunz de sable'.

   S. M. Collins, F.S.A., notes 'Sir Jon Revel' with arms as above in Powell's Roll, c. 1350
(Oxford, Bodleian Library, MS. Ashmole, 804, IV, fo. 20b), 'William Revell' with the same
in the Antiquaries' Roll, c. 1355 (Society of Antiquaries' MS. 136, Part I, fo. 7b), and
'Perus Maulorie' with arms as above in Erdeswicke's Roll, c. 1295.

Plate XIII

58

SIR JOHN FORTESCUE, CHIEF JUSTICE OF THE KING'S BENCH

Born about 1394, died about 1476

Azure a bend engrailed argent cotised or

His seal (Lord Clermont, Life and Works of Sir John Fortescue, 1869, Vol. I, p. 25);
Visitation of Devon, 1620; College of Arms MS. L.2 (c. 1530) blazons '*Fortescu beryth
asur a bende ingrayled silver cotesed gold*'. Harl. MS. 6163, fo. 120b (Foster, Two Tudor
Books of Arms, p. 303) gives Sir John Fortescue this coat with a mullet pierced sable on
the bend for cadency.

Plate XIII

59

SIR THOMAS LITTLETON
Born 1422, died 1481

Argent a chevron between three escallops sable

These Arms with others were before the Civil War on Sir Thomas's tomb in Worcester
Cathedral (William Thomas, 'A Survey of the Cathedral Church of Worcester', 1737,
p. 113), and that they were used by him is shown by their impalement with those of Burley
for his wife Joan, daughter of Sir William Burley. His paternal coat, which he abandoned,
was, *Argent a bend cotised sable within a border gules bezany,* for Westcote of Devonshire
(shown on the tomb impaling Littleton), he being son of Thomas Westcote by Elizabeth
daughter and heir of Thomas Littleton of Frankley, Worcestershire. He succeeded to his
mother's estates and took the name and Arms of her family, while his younger brothers
retained those of Westcote.

Plate XIII

60

WILLIAM OF WAYNFLETE, BISHOP OF WINCHESTER
Born about 1395, died 1486

Lozengy ermine and sable on a chief of the second three lilies argent
slipped and seeded or

These Arms are on his tomb in Winchester Cathedral and were adopted by his foundation
Magdalen College, Oxford. He was son of Richard Patten of Wainfleet, Lincolnshire, and
since the Pattens in the sixteenth century bore *Lozengy ermine and sable* (Coll. Arm. MS.
Vincent 183, fo. 92b), it is conjectured that William added the chief of lilies to his paternal
coat in allusion to the Arms of Eton College of which he was the second Provost.

XII

49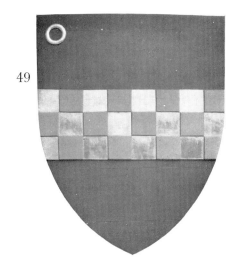

50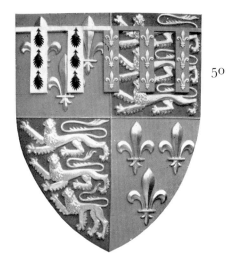

51

52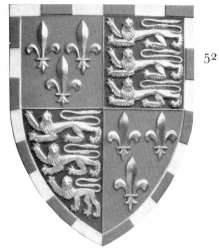

54

55

64

1521

1598

WILLIAM CECIL. BARON OF BURGHLEY.
KNIGHT OF THE GARTER.

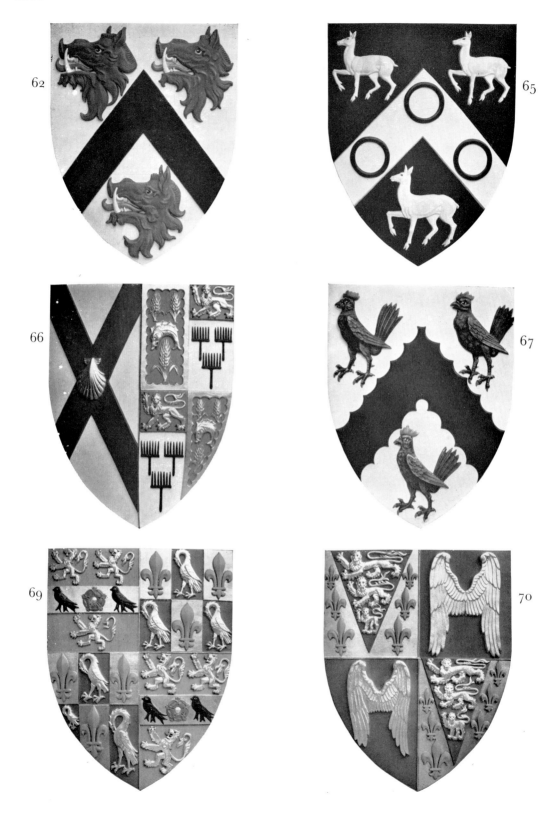

Plate XIII

61

MARGARET BEAUFORT, COUNTESS OF RICHMOND AND DERBY
Born 1443, died 1509

PER PALE

Dexter. EDMUND TUDOR, EARL OF RICHMOND

>*Quarterly,* 1 *and* 4, FRANCE MODERN, *Azure three fleurs de lys or*
>2 *and* 3, ENGLAND, *Gules three leopards or*

All within a bordure azure charged with fleurs de lys and martlets or

Sinister. BEAUFORT

>*Quarterly,* 1 *and* 4, FRANCE MODERN, *Azure three fleurs de lys or*
>2 *and* 3, ENGLAND, *Gules three leopards or*

All within a bordure gobony argent and azure

This impaled Coat appears (as does another impalement for her third marriage with Lord Derby) on her tomb at Westminster Abbey (Historical Monuments Commission, London, Vol. I, p. 68); the Beaufort Arms alone on her Seal (Sandford, Genealogical History, p. 328), and carved in stone at Christ's and St. John's Colleges, Cambridge (St. John Hope, Heraldry for Craftsmen and Designers, pp. 395, 396).

Plate XVI

62

WILLIAM ELPHINSTONE, BISHOP OF ABERDEEN AND FOUNDER OF ABERDEEN UNIVERSITY
Born 1431, died 1514

Argent a chevron between three boars' heads erased sable

Shown on his Seal (Laing, Scottish Seals, 1850, No. 898 and Supp., 1866, No. 1031; Birch, British Museum Seals, No. 14983), in the corner of his portrait at Aberdeen University (Spalding Club, Fasti Aberdonenses, 1854, frontispiece) and on a carving in oak there (Edinburgh Heraldic Exhibition Catalogue, 1892, No. 228, Pl. LII).

Plate XIV

63

THOMAS WOLSEY, CARDINAL AND LEGATE, BISHOP OF DURHAM AND WINCHESTER
Born about 1472, died 1530

SHIELD. *Sable on a cross engrailed argent a lion passant gules between four leopards' faces azure, on a chief or a rose gules barbed and seeded proper between two Cornish choughs sable beaked and legged gules*

In front of a legatine and an archiepiscopal cross in saltire and surmounted by a Cardinal's hat

SUPPORTERS. *Two griffins per fess gules and argent, wings elevated, beaks, ears and tufts or*

MOTTO. *Dominus mihi adiutor*

Sir William Dethick, Garter, in his 'Answers' to certain charges made against him in 1602 (Coll. Arm. MS. WZ, fo. 274) stated that Sir Thomas Wriothesley, Garter, joined with Thomas Benolt, Clarenceux, 'in a patent of armes to Cardinall Woolsey. 18. H. 8'. College of Arms MS. L.10, fo. 69 (c. 1520-30) gives this coat five times over impaled with the Arms of the Sees of York, Durham, Bath and Wells, Salisbury, and Winchester. The Parliamentary Roll of 1523 (Heralds' Commemorative Exhibition, 1484-1934, No. 14, Pl. 30) shows it impaled with the See of York. The present design is based on a carving at Hampton Court (Historical Monuments Commission, Middlesex, Pl. 78) and a painting reproduced in 'Examples of Armorial Bookplates', Second Series, W. Griggs & Sons, 1892. It was reasonably conjectured by Everard Green, Somerset Herald (The Nineteenth Century, June 1896) that we see in Wolsey's Arms 'the sable shield and cross engrailed of the Uffords, Earls of Suffolk'; Wolsey being son of an Ipswich butcher; 'in the azure leopards' faces those of the coat of De la Pole, Earls of Suffolk; in the purple lion, the badge of Pope Leo X; in the rose, the Lancastrian sympaties of the builder of Cardinal's College (Christ Church) Oxford; and in the choughs, the reputed or assigned Arms of St. Thomas of Canterbury—argent three choughs proper. Thus in the cardinal's coat we see his county and its history (i.e. its two earldoms), his religion and his politics, his Christian name and his patron saint.' His coat has become that of Christ Church, Oxford.

63

DOMINVS MIHI ADIVTOR

1472

1530

THOMAS WOLSEY. CARDINAL. & LEGATE
DE LATERE . ARCHBISHOP OF YORK.

Plate XV

64

WILLIAM CECIL, BARON OF BURGHLEY, KNIGHT OF THE GARTER

Born 1520, died 1598

Quarterly of 6. 1 *and* 6, Cecil. *Barry of ten argent and azure six escucheons sable, three, two and one, each charged with a lion rampant of the first*

2, Winstone. *Per pale gules and azure a lion rampant argent sustaining a tree eradicated vert*

3, Caerleon. *Sable a plate between three towers triple towered ports open argent*

4, Heckington. *Argent on a bed cotised gules three cinquefoils or*

5, Walcot. *Argent a chevron between three chess rooks ermines*

Within the Garter

CREST. *On a closed helmet in profile, and wreath argent and sable, A garb or supported by two lions the dexter azure the sinister argent*

MANTLING. *Gules and argent*

SUPPORTERS. *On either side a lion rampant ermine*

MOTTO. *Cor unum via una*

Nos. 1, 2 and 3, and the Crest, were allowed to William Scicill of Allt yr ynis at the Visitation of Herefordshire 1569. The marriage with the Winston heiress (herself shown as grand-daughter of the Caerleon heiress) five generations back is shadowy. Burghley's claim that his grandfather David Cecil was a younger son of this family of small gentry is thought not impossible by Oswald Barron (Northamptonshire Families, Victoria County Histories, 1906, p. 22). David's son Richard married Jane, daughter of Richard Heckington of Bourne by Alice, daughter of Robert Walcot. Her Arms are on her monument at St. Martin's, Stamford. Burghley's Achievement is taken from his Garter Stall Plate, except the Motto, which is from his monument at Stamford.

Plate XVI

65

JOHN COLET, DEAN OF ST. PAUL'S
Born about 1467, died 1519

Sable on a chevron between three hinds trippant argent three annulets of the field

Harl. MS. 6163, fo. 121b (Foster, Two Tudor Books of Arms, p. 303) for 'Sir Harry Colett, Maior of London', the Dean's father. There is a double pun. The hind is 'Colette', feminine of 'Colin' the stag; and the annulets are 'collets' (information from Oswald Barron, F.S.A., Maltravers Herald Extraordinary). Foster mistakenly attempts a different pun by making the hinds 'colts'.

Plate XVI

66

JOHN FISHER, BISHOP OF ROCHESTER
Born 1459, died 1535

PER PALE. *Dexter*, SEE OF ROCHESTER. *Argent on a saltire gules an escallop or*
Sinister. Quarterly, 1 and 4, FISHER. *Azure a dolphin embowed between three ears of barley within a border engrailed or*
2 and 3, *Argent three eel spears, tynes upward, sable, on a chief azure a leopard or*

Shown thus in the Parliamentary Roll for 1523 (Catalogue of the Heralds' Commemorative Exhibition 1484-1934, No. 14, Pl. XXX), and in a contemporary manuscript in the College of Arms (L.10, fo. 93b).

Plate XVI

67

SIR THOMAS MORE
Born 1478, died 1535

Argent a chevron engrailed between three moorcocks sable crested gules

Harl. MS. 6163, fo. 105 (Foster, Two Tudor Books of Arms, p. 294). Probably granted to Sir John More, father of Sir Thomas, temp. Edward IV, cf. Wriothesley's Roll of Grants (Archaeologia, Vol. 69, p. 74, No. 80). Carved (with a Quartering) on a capital and tomb in Chelsea Old Church (Historical Monuments Commission, London, Vol. II, pp. 8, 9).

68

WILLIAM TYNDALE
Translator of the Bible. Died 1536

(probably) *Argent on a fess gules between three garbs sable a martlet or*

Given as the Arms of Thomas Tyndall of Eastwood, Co. Gloucester, who 'deceased at Master Pennes House in London the XXVIIIth daye of Aprile in Ao. Dom. 1571', on his Funeral Certificate. B. W. Greenfield (Genealogy of the Family of Tyndale, 1842) showed that this Thomas was son of Edward Tyndale of Pull Court in Slimbridge, Co. Gloucester, receiver of Lord Berkeley's lands in 1519. E. C. Waters (The Chesters of Chicheley, p. 277) states that Greenfield 'has since discovered from a letter of Bishop Stokesley in the Record Office that . . . Edward Tyndale . . . was the brother of William Tyndale the Reformer'.

Plate XVI   69

THOMAS CROMWELL, EARL OF ESSEX
Born about 1485, died 1540

Quarterly. 1 *and* 4, CROMWELL. *Azure on a fess between three lions rampant or a rose gules barbed and seeded proper between two martlets sable*

2 *and* 3, *Party of six pieces or and gules three fleurs de lys azure and three pelicans or*

Parliament Roll for 1539/40 (College of Arms, Box 40, Roll 40; Heralds' Commemorative Exhibition Catalogue, No. 15, Pl. XXX), where the Arms are struck through with a note 'traditur'.

Plate XVI   70

EDWARD SEYMOUR, DUKE OF SOMERSET, PROTECTOR
OF THE REALM
Born 1500, died 1552

Quarterly. 1 *and* 4, AUGMENTATION. *Or on a pile gules between six fleurs de lys azure three leopards of the field*

2 *and* 3, SEYMOUR. *Gules a pair of wings inverted conjoined in lure or*

The Seymour Coat appears in Harl. MS. 6163, fo. 101b (c. 1480-1500; Foster, Two Tudor Books of Arms, pp. 286-7) for 'Sir John Seymore', and quartered with the Augmentation (which is based on the arms of France and England) for the Protector in a contemporary collection of paintings of Arms of Knights of the Garter (Coll. Arm. MS. M.7, fo. 40b).

Plate XVII

71

THOMAS CRANMER, ARCHBISHOP OF CANTERBURY
Born 1489, died 1556

PER PALE

Dexter. THE SEE OF CANTERBURY. *Azure an archiepiscopal staff or surmounted by a pall argent fringed and charged with four crosses formy fitchy of the second*

Sinister. Quarterly, 1 *and* 4, CRANMER. *Argent on a chevron azure between three pelicans sable three cinquefoils pierced or*

2, (probably meant for Aslacton) *Gules six lions rampant argent crowned and within a border or*

3, ASLACTON. *Argent five fusils in fess gules each charged with an escallop or*

Parliament Roll of 1539/40 (College for Arms, Box 40, Roll 40; Herald's Commemorative Exhibition Catalogue, No. 15, Pl. XXX). R. E. Chester Waters (Genealogical Memoirs of the Chesters of Chicheley, 1878, Vol. II, pp. 383, 425) infers that the Coat in the first quarter was granted to Cranmer by Christopher Barker, Garter in 1539 or 1540, in lieu of his paternal Coat of three cranes. The Archbishop's great-grandfather Edmund Cranmer married Isabel, daughter and heir of William de Aslacton, and acquired with her the manor of Aslacton, Co. Nottingham. The second quarter is probably intended for Aslacton on a mistaken assumption of identity with the Yorkshire family of Haslarton. The Parliamentary Roll, c. 1310, gives '*Sire Thomas de Haselartone, de goules a iij lioncels de argent coronez de or*'.

Plate XVII

72

SIR PHILIP SIDNEY
Born 1554, died 1586

Or a pheon azure

Shown on the banners carried at the funeral of his father Sir Henry Sidney (Coll. Arm. MS., Dethick's Funerals of Nobility, Vol. I, p. 3b), and on the engraved roll of his own funeral procession by Thomas Lant (Heralds' Commemorative Exhibition Catalogue, 1484-1934, No. 9, Pl. XV). These Arms first appear in 1451 on a Seal of William Sydney of Kingsham, whose father, William of Cranlegh, sealed with a letter W, of which it has been conjectured that the pheon may be simply an elaboration (Archaeologia, Vol. 65, p. 252, C. L. Kingsford, 'On some ancient deeds and seals belonging to Lord de L'Isle and Dudley'; Sussex Archaeological Collections, Vol. 59, p. 34, L. F. Salzmann, Canting Arms in Sussex).

For an exact parallel in eighteenth century Denmark see Poul-Bredo Grandjean, Initiales cachées dans quelques armoiries bourgeoises, Revue française d'héraldique et de sigillographie, Tome I, 1938, pp. 73-6.

College of Arms MS. L.1 (c. 1540) blazons *Sydney beryth gold a brode arrow hed asur the point downward*.

73
SIR FRANCIS WALSINGHAM
Born about 1530, died 1590

Paly of six argent and sable a fess gules
A crescent for cadency

Allowed at the Visitations of Kent 1574 and 1619 to Sir Thomas Walsingham of Scadbury in Chiselhurst, whose father was elder brother of William, father of Sir Francis.

Plate XVII

74
SIR JOHN HAWKINS
Born 1532, died 1595

Sable on a point wavy argent and azure a lion passant or, in chief three
bezants, and for Augmentation, on a canton or an escallop between two
palmers' staves sable

Arms 'goven and graunted ratyfyed and confirmed' to John Hawkins and the other descendants of his father William Hawkins of Plymouth, by William Hervy, Clarenceux, 1 March 1565, 'in consideracion of the prowes and vertue manyfestly apperinge in the said John Hawkins', 'forasmuch as the coragious woorthy and famous entreprises begonne atchieved and done by the skell and travaile of John Hawkins of Plimmouthe in the county of Devon Esquier into the unhaunted partes of Affrica and America have bin suche wherby

71

his highe and comendable service towardes this his naturall countery the realme of Englande hath well meryted and deserved to have some woorthy signe and token in Armes for perpetuall memory therof. Althoughe that the said John Hawkins is lyneally descended from his auncestors a gent'; being '*Sables on a poynte wave a lyon passaunt goulde in chiefe iij bezantz*'. Augmentation granted c. 1569 by Robert Cooke, Clarenceux, 'for a perpetuall memory' of the fact that Hawkins 'travaylinge to the West Indias in Ao 1568 arryved at a towne caled Rio de la Hacha nere Capo de la Vela to thende to furnyshe him self of suche necessaryes as he wanted viz. water and fuell where he was by Michell de Castilianos a Spanyard in warlyke wise resisted with 100 harkabushers, nevertheles the sayd John Hawkins with 200 men under his conduction and valiantnes entered the sayd towne and not only put the sayd captayne and his men to flight but also toke and brought his enseigne away'; being, '*On a canton golde a skalop betwen two palmers staves sables*'. In modern practice the canton would eclipse the dexter bezant, but Coll. Arm. MS. Misc. Gts., I, 148, shows them as here. The 1565 Coat suggests the English lion bestriding the waves and bringing back treasure of bezants. The escallop and palmers' staves are emblems of pilgrimage.

Plate *XVII*

75

SIR FRANCIS DRAKE
Born about 1540, died 1596

Sable a fess wavy between two stars argent

Assigned and given by Queen Elizabeth, being pleased 'graciously to regard the praysworthie deseartes of Sir Francys Drake knight and to remunerate the same in him', as recited in a Patent of Robert Cooke, Clarenceux, dated 21 June 1581, blazoning the shield '*Of sable a fece wavy betweene two starres argent*', and the crest, granted at the same time, '*A globe terrestriall, upon the height wherof, in a shyppe under sayle, trayned aboute the same with golden haulsers by the direction of a hand appeeringe owte of the cloudes, all yn proper colour, a read dragon volant shewith it self regardinge the said direction, with these wordes Auxilio divino*'. The shield alludes (as does the crest) to the circumnavigation of the globe

Plate *XVII*

76

RICHARD HOOKER
Born about 1554, died 1600

Or a fess vair between two leopards sable, a crescent for cadency

Allowed at the Visitation of Devon 1572 to John Vowell *alias* Hooker of Exeter, whose younger brother Roger was father of Richard. J. L. Vivian (The Visitations of the County of Devon, 1895, p. 479) derives the *alias* name from an early Vowell-Hooker marriage.

81

1599

1658

OLIVER CROMWELL·LORD PROTECTOR
OF ENGLAND·SCOTLAND·AND IRELAND

82

FIEL · PERO · DESDICHADO

1650   1722

JOHN CHURCHILL. DUKE OF MARLBOROUGH
KNIGHT OF THE GARTER

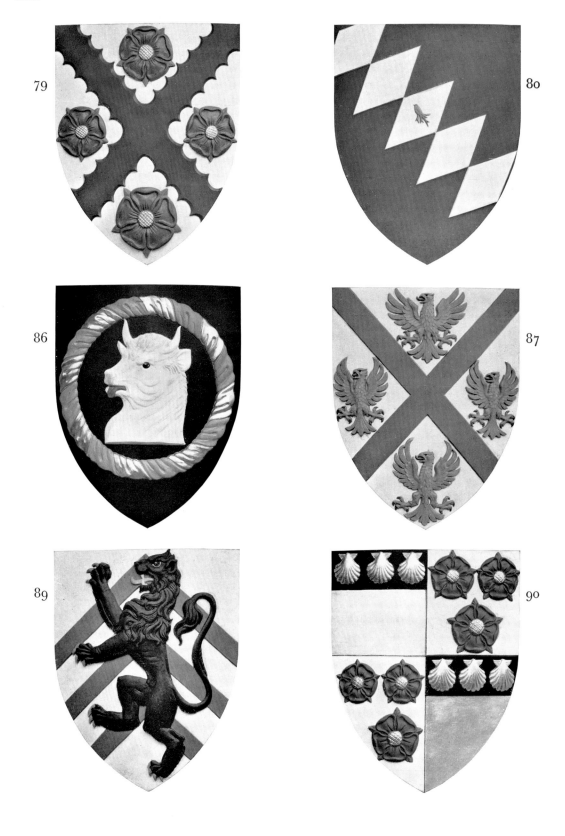

77

ROBERT DEVEREUX, EARL OF ESSEX
Born 1566, died 1601

Argent a fess gules in chief three torteaux

Shown in a contemporary manuscript of 'Arms and Descents of the Nobility' in the College of Arms. L.1 (c. 1540) blazons *'Devereux beryth silver a fece geules in the chief three torteaulx'*. Glover's Roll (c. 1245) blazons a counterchanged version of this ancient Coat, *'William de Evereux, de goules ove ung fesse d'argent et trois torteaulx d'argent en le cheif'*.

Plate XVII

78

WILLIAM SHAKESPEARE
Born 1564, died 1616

Or on a bend sable a spear of the first the point steeled proper

Arms granted 20 Oct. 1596 by Sir William Dethick, Garter King of Arms, to John Shake-speare of Stratford-on-Avon, father of William, *'Gould on a bend sable a speare of the first the poynt steeled proper'* (Heralds' Commemorative Exhibition Catalogue, Nos. 18, 19 and Pl. XXXVIII).

Plate XX

79

JOHN NAPIER OF MERCHISTON
Born 1550, died 1617

Argent a saltire engrailed between four roses gules

Given for 'Napar of Marcheinstown' in Sir David Lyndsay of the Mount's manuscript (1542; ed. Laing, 1878, p. 92); on John Napier's own Seal (Laing, Scottish Seals, 1850, No. 626); and on those of his ancestors from 1453 (ib. No. 621) or earlier.

Plate XX

80

SIR WALTER RALEIGH
Born about 1552, died 1618

Gules five lozenges in bend argent, the middle lozenge charged with a martlet for cadency

Allowed at the Heralds' Visitations of Devon 1530 and Wiltshire 1623. College of Arms MS. L.2 blazons '*Rale of Devon beryth geules v lozenges in bend silver*'; cf. an earlier blazon of this coat in the Parliamentary Roll, '*Sire Simon de Ralee de goules a une bende engrele de argent*'. It is doubtless derived through tenure or kinship from that of Marshal, Barons Marshal, *Gules a bend engrailed or* (see No. 8, and Smith Ellis, Antiquities of Heraldry, p. 203).

Plate XVIII

81

OLIVER CROMWELL, LORD PROTECTOR OF ENGLAND SCOTLAND AND IRELAND
Born 1599, died 1658

SHIELD. *Quarterly*, 1 *and* 4, ENGLAND (*St. George*). *Argent a cross gules*
2, SCOTLAND (*St. Andrew*). *Azure a saltire argent*
3, IRELAND. *Azure a harp or stringed argent*
In pretence, CROMWELL. *Sable a lion rampant argent*

CREST (on a crowned Royal helmet). *A lion statant guardant imperially crowned or*

MANTLING. *Sable and ermine*

SUPPORTERS. *Dexter, for England. A lion rampant guardant imperially crowned or*
Sinister, for Wales. A dragon with wings elevated gules purfled or

MOTTO. *Pax quaeritur bello*

The design is taken from the Protector's Great Seal (Wyon, Great Seals of England, p. 95, Pl. 32; St. John Hope, Heraldry for Craftsmen and Designers, p. 404), and the colourings with some necessary corrections of obvious slips, from the following description in Prestwich's *Respublica* (1787, p. 20) of the display at the Protector's Installation. 'On a prince-like shield, fashioned as a royal breast-plate, four flags borne quarterly, viz. in the first and fourth, the Cross of St. George, the Patron of England, which is blazoned thus, Gules, a plain cross argent. 2d, the extended cross, or Saltier, called the Cross of St. Andrew, Patron of Scotland or North Britain, blazoned azure, a cross Saltier Argent. 3d, the Harp of Ireland, called King David's Harp, blazoned azure, a lyre of gold with strings of silver. The fourth quarter as the first above-mentioned: and over all, in fess, on a Saxon-fashioned shield of a knight, the paternal arms of his Highness Oliver Cromwell, viz. Argent a lion rampant Sable [*sic*]. The whole timbred with a princely helmet of steel, burnished with gold and mantled Sable on each side, treble lamberquin'd and lined with ermine. At top of this and helmet a princely crown of gold, etc. on the top of which, the royal crest of Great Britain, which is a lion passant guardant Or, crowned with an imperial crown of gold. Supporters, 1st, a lion guardant and imperially crowned, the supporter of England, Or. 2d, a dragon in profile, with wings raised and indorsed Vert [*sic*], purfled with gold, for ancient Britain or Wales. Motto, PAX QUAERITUR BELLO, that is, Peace sought by War.'

The banner of St. George was among those borne by the English army at the siege of Caerlaverock in 1300 (line 947). A figure of St. Andrew was placed on their Great Seal by the Guardians of Scotland (1286-92; Birch, British Museum Seals, No. 14790). The harp appears as the crest of Ireland among the crests of Edward IV shown in the Warwick Roll (c. 1480), but a late thirteenth-century French Roll of Arms now in Holland gives *Or a harp gules* for *Le Roy d'Irlande* (Antiquaries' Journal, Vol. XXI. p. 209).

The Cromwell Coat, allowed at the Visitation of Northamptonshire and Huntingdonshire, 1564, to Sir Henry Cromwell *alias* Williams, grandfather of Oliver, may be based on that attributed to Elystan Glodrydd, Prince of Ferlex, the Welsh patriarch from whom the pedigree is deduced, *Gules a lion rampant or*.

Plate XIX

82

JOHN CHURCHILL, DUKE OF MARLBOROUGH
KNIGHT OF THE GARTER
Born 1650, died 1722

SHIELD. *Quarterly,* 1, CHURCHILL. *Sable a lion rampant argent on a canton of the second a cross gules*

2, WILDIARDE. *Azure four bendlets argent and a bordure or*

3, TILLE. *Argent a fess per fess indented throughout or and gules*

4, WINSTON. *Per pale gules and azure a lion rampant argent supporting a tree eradicated vert*

Within the Garter

CREST. *On a Peer's helmet, within a Ducal coronet, on a wreath argent and sable, A lion couchant guardant argent supporting with the dexter paw a banner gules charged with a dexter hand argent the staff or*

MANTLING. *Gules and ermine*

SUPPORTERS. *On either side a wyvern gules*

MOTTO. *Fiel pero desdichado*

This design is based on his Garter Stall Plate. The crest and the canton of augmentation in the first quarter with permission to 'leave out the bend' from his Arms were granted to Sir Winston Churchill, the Duke's father, by Sir Edward Walker, Garter, 20 Jan. 1661/2, in virtue of a Royal Warrant of 5 Dec. 1661 (Calendar of State Papers Domestic, 1661/2, p. 176) for his service to the late King as Captain of the Horse and present loyalty as a member of the House of Commons. The Arms of Sir Winston's father, John Churchill of the Middle Temple, who married Sara, daughter and heir of Sir Henry Winston of Standish, Co. Gloucester, in 1618, are given in a pedigree of Bond, recorded in the College of Arms in 1669, as *'Sable a lion rampant argent debruised by a bend gules'.* This coat was allowed at the Visitation of Dorset in 1623 to William Churchill of Muston, and it is not unlikely that John may descend from a branch of this family (see Hutchins, History of Dorset, Vol. IV, p. 471). The pedigree deriving him from a Norman origin, given in Collins' Peerage and elsewhere, in virtue of which the Wildiarde and Tille quarterings are claimed, is, like these quarterings, fictitious (cf. Hutchins, *supra* cit. and Family Origins, by the late J. H. Round, ed. William Page, 1930, pp. 33-42, The Origin of the Churchills). Sir Henry Wynston's Arms are entered in the 1623 Visitation of Gloucestershire, where his pedigree is derived from a common origin with the Winstons whose Arms are quartered by Lord Burleigh (No. 64)

FRANCIS BACON, VISCOUNT SAINT ALBANS
Born 1561, died 1626

Gules on a chief argent two mullets sable
For cadency a crescent (charged with an annulet)

The Parliamentary Roll (c. 1310) gives, under Hampshire, '*Sire Edmoun Bacoun, de goules od la chef argent a ij moles sable*'. And this coat, '*Goules on a chiefe argent two mullettes sables*', was in 1568 confirmed to Sir Nicholas Bacon, the Lord Keeper, by Sir Gilbert Dethick, Garter, on the insufficient strength of 'his old wrytinges and certayne auncient bookes somtyme pertayninge to the Abbay of Bury Sanct Edmond in the County of Suff. togeather with divers coppies of recordes remayning in the tower of London', although Christopher Barker, Garter 1536-1550, had a few years earlier granted him a new coat, *Azure on a fess between three fleurs de lys or three griffins' heads of the field.* This coat is entered in the 1561 Visitation of Suffolk, but has later been struck through. Francis was fifth son of Sir Nicholas, who was a second son. I find him using his father's mark of cadency only (College of Arms MS., Walker's Nobility, p. 285).

84
SIR EDWARD COKE, CHIEF JUSTICE
Born 1549, died 1633

Per pale gules and azure three eagles displayed argent claws counterchanged

Shown thus on Sir Edward Coke's Funeral Certificate.

85
THOMAS WENTWORTH, EARL OF STAFFORD
Born 1593, died 1641

Sable a chevron between three leopard's faces or

Allowed to William Wentworth of Wentworth Woodhouse, Yorkshire, at the Visitation of the North, 1530.

Plate XX

86

JOHN PYM
Born 1584, died 1643

Sable a bull's head couped argent witin a wreath azure and or

These Arms are given for John Pym's family, Pym of Brymore, in a pedigree dated 1583 in Harl. MS. 1385 (fo. 21) which purports to be a copy of a Visitation of Somerset made mainly in 1573-4. There is no original in the College of Arms, but Philipot MS. 38 there purports to be another copy, and gives the Pym pedigree (continued to 1644) with the same Arms; and Le Neve, in his Baronets' Pedigrees (Vol. III, p. 129) in the College refers to a like entry in a third copy 'amongst my Lord Anglesey's books'. Collinson (History of Somerset, 1791, Vo!. I, p. 233) states that this coat was borne by Philip Pym in the reign of Edward IV.

Plate XX

87

JOHN HAMPDEN
Born 1594, died 1643

Argent a saltire gules between four eagles displayed azure

Allowed to John Hampden at the Visitation of Buckinghamshire 1634. The pedigree (in the College of Arms) then entered bears his signature. The Arms are on a seal of John Hampden, 1431 (Birch, British Museum Seals, No. 10448; attached to Harl. Ch. 51, C. 46).

88

WILLIAM LAUD, ARCHBISHOP OF CANTERBURY
Born 1573, died 1645

PER PALE. *Dexter*, SEE OF CANTERBURY. *Azure the cross staff of an archbishop in pale or surmounted of a pall proper*
Sinister, LAUD. *Sable on a chevron between three estoiles or three crosses paty fitchy gules*

Granted by William Camden, Clarenceux, to Laud when Bishop elect of St. David's (1621).

Plate XX

89

JOHN WINTHROP, GOVERNOR OF MASSACHUSETTS
Born 1588, died 1649

Argent three chevrons gules over all a lion rampant sable armed and langued azure

Granted 24 June 1592 by William Dethick, Garter, to John Wynthrope, the colonist's uncle, for himself and the other descendants of his father Adam Wynthrope of Groton, Co. Suffolk; blazoned *'d'argent three cheverons gules over all a lyon rampant sables armed & langued azure'*.

Plate XX

90

JAMES GRAHAM, MARQUESS OF MONTROSE
Born 1612, died 1650

Quarterly, 1 and 4, GRAHAM. *Or on a chief sable three escallops of the first*
2 and 3, MONTROSE. *Argent three roses gules barbed and seeded proper*

Given thus in a manuscript of the reign of Charles I in the College of Arms (E.D.N. Scotland's Nobility, p. 34) for 'The earle of Mountroshe and Lord Graham'. The first quarter appears (of course without tinctures) c. 1250 on the Seal of Sir Nicholas Graham (Laing, Scottish Seals, 1850, No. 373; Scots Peerage, Vol. VI, pp. 194-5), and, as *Argent on a chief sable three escallops or*, c. 1340 in the Balliol Roll (Coll. Arm. MS. Vincent 164, fo. 110b). The canting coat for Montrose appears on the second Earl's seal in 1541 (Laing, *supra*, No. 385).

91

WILLIAM HARVEY
Born 1578, died 1657

Or on a chief indented sable three crescents argent

College of Arms MS. E.D.N. 57, fo. 461, records these Arms for 'Sir Daniel Harvey of Comb Nevil in Surrey Kt', son of William's brother Daniel; and a recorded Pedigree (2nd

14, fo. 115) D. assigns them to Mary wife of William Whitmore, daughter of his brother Eliab. Hence it may probably be inferred (despite the omission of Arms from the Pedigree recorded at the 1634 Visitation of London) that the limitations of whatever grant or allowance was made extended to all the descendants of William's father, Thomas Harvey, for whose burial at Hackney in June 1623 a 'Painter's Work Book' (O.I., fo. 23) in the College of Arms records the provision of '1 dozen of scucheons' of this coat, by Mr. Philpott.

92
ROBERT BLAKE, ADMIRAL
Born 1598, died 1657

Argent a chevron between three garbs sable

Allowed to Robert Blake of Calne, third cousin once removed to the Admiral, at the Visitation of Wiltshire 1565, and to Humphrey Blake of Bridgwater, his brother, at the Visitation of Somerset 1672. The Pedigree of Robert Blake of London, son of Robert of Stowey, probably a kinsman, entered in 1633, has this note: 'The armes respited for 6 monthes & then to pay fees'.

Plate XXI

93
JOHN MILTON
Born 1608, died 1674

Argent a double headed eagle displayed gules beaked and legged azure

A Patent of confirmation of these Arms with the grant of a Crest, by Sir William Segar, Garter, to 'Mylton *alias* Mytton of . . . Co. Oxford', is recorded. This is undoubtedly John Milton's father, who named his inn in Bread Street the Spread Eagle. A 'Painter's Work Book' in the College of Arms (I.B.7, fo. 46b) records the use of these Arms at 'the funerall of Secretary Milton his wife her name Woodcock' in 1658. The coat is based, without historical justification, on that of Mytton of Shropshire.

80

94

EDWARD HYDE, EARL OF CLARENDON
Born 1609, died 1674

Azure a chevron between three lozenges or

In Ballard's 'Visitation' of Cheshire, c. 1480 (Coll. Arm. MS. M.3, fo. 3b), 'Hamont Hyde', Lord Clarendon's great-great-great-grandfather, '*berithe asure a cheveron betwene iij losengis golde*'; and his father, Henry Hyde of Purton, was entered in 1623 at the Visitation of Wiltshire.

Plate XXI

95

JOHN DRYDEN, POET LAUREATE
Born 1631, died 1700

Azure a lion rampant and in chief a sphere between two estoiles or
For cadency a mullet

Entered 3 March 1630 on the Funeral Certificate of Anne, wife of Sir John Dryden, Baronet, of Canons Ashby, Co. Northampton, the poet's uncle, and allowed at the Visitation of Northamptonshire 1681. Erasmus, the poet's father, was third son of Sir Erasmus Dryden.

Plate XXI

96

SAMUEL PEPYS
Born 1632, died 1703

Sable on a bend or between two horses' heads erased argent three fleurs de lys of the field
For cadency a crescent

Allowed to Thomas Pepys of South Creake at the Visitation of Norfolk 1561. Samuel was great-grandson of John Pepys of Cottenham, Co. Cambridge, second son of Thomas' uncle. For the rise of this family see F. M. Page, Estates of Crowland Abbey, Cambridge, 1934.

Plate XXI

97

WILLIAM PENN, QUAKER AND FOUNDER OF PENNSYLVANIA
Born 1644, died 1718

Argent on a fess sable three plates

Allowed at the Visitation of Buckinghamshire 1634 to William Penn's father. The Parliamentary Roll (c. 1310) blazons '*Sire Johan de la Penne, de argent a une fesse de sable en la fesse iij rondels de argent*'. The manor of Penn, Buckinghamshire, 'has continued in the Penn family ... but the links between the members of this family holding from the 13th to the 16th century have not been clearly established' (Victoria County History, Buckinghamshire, Vol. III, p. 237).

Plate XXI

98

SIR CHRISTOPHER WREN
Born 1632, died 1723

Argent a chevron between three lions' heads erased sable on a chief gules three cross crosslets or

Glover's Visitation of Durham 1575, records the grant in that year by William Flower, Norroy, probably to Anthony Wrenne of Billyhall or Sherbornhouse, of *Argent on a chevron azure between three lions' heads erased purpure three wrens argent, on a chief gules three cross crosslets or*. The 1615 Visitation of Durham gives this coat for Anthony's son, Sir Charles Wrenn of Binchester, with the lions' heads azure and the wrens omitted. The Funeral Certificate (1667) of Matthew Wren, Bishop of Ely, first cousin once removed to Anthony, and uncle to Sir Christopher, further changes both chevrons and lions' heads to sable, and is followed by the 1684 Visitation of Cambridgeshire. These variations might perhaps be explained by the progressive obfuscation of an original exemplar.

Plate XXII

99
ROBERT WALPOLE, EARL OF ORFORD, KNIGHT OF THE GARTER
Born 1676, died 1745

SHIELD. *Or on a fess between two chevronels sable three cross crosslets of the field Within the Garter*

CREST. *On a Peer's helmet, within an Earl's coronet, on a wreath of the colours, the bust of a man in profile ducally crowned proper with a long cap pointing forwards gules charged with a Catherine Wheel and the tassel or*

MANTLING. *Gules and ermine*

SUPPORTERS. *On the dexter side an antelope argent attired proper ungled or and gorged with a collar eschequeté ermine and gules with a golden chain affixed thereunto passing between his fore leggs and reflexed over his back, and on the sinister side an hart argent attired proper ungled and gorged with a like collar and chain as the same are depicted in the margin.*

MOTTO. *Fari quae sentiat*

Based on the Garter Stall Plate but omitting the quarterings and substituting a Peer's helmet. The shield appears in this form on the seal of Henry de Walpole in 1408 (Collins's Peerage of England, ed. Sir E. Brydges, 1812, Vol. V, p. 639) and Sir Henry de Walpole of Houghton, Norfolk, in the reign of Henry III, 'sealed, as by his deed appears, with a fess between two chevrons' (Collins's Peerage of England, ed. Sir E. Brydges, 1812, Vol. V, p. 635; Blomefield, History of Norfolk, 1769, Vol. VI, p. 796). The crosslets might have become obliterated through wear. The coat is presumably based on that of the Fitzwalters (*Or a fess between two chevrons gules*; No. 12), who were great lords in Norfolk and near Walpole (Book of Fees, 1920-31, pp. 576, 629-30), from which place the Walpole family no doubt derived, though its connection with the early Walpoles holding there is unproved (Family origins, by the late J. H. Round, ed. William Page, 1930, pp. 43-53, The Origin of the Walpoles). The Fitzwalter Coat in turn derives from that of the Clares (see No. 4), *Or three chevrons gules*, of whom the Fitzwalters were a branch. Rye (Coat Armour used in Norfolk before 1563, Pt. II, 1918, pp. 93-4) tries to derive the arms of both Walpole and Fitzwalter from those of Baynard (of Norfolk and Baynard's Castle, London), *Sable a fess between two chevrons or*, but it is far more likely that Baynard like Walpole derives from Fitzwalter, Fulk Baynard being returned as Robert Fitzwalter's late tenant in 1236 (Book of Fees, Vol. I, p. 576).

The Arms were allowed at the 1563 Visitation of Norfolk, the Crest at that of 1664, and the Supporters were granted to Sir Robert as a Knight of the Bath by John Anstis, Garter, 15 July 1725. The crest is evidently derived from that of Robsart, *A soldan's head argent crined azure wearing a crown or and cap gules surmounted by a Catherine Wheel or and vert*, which appears on the Garter Stall Plate of Sir Lewis Robsart, K.G. (d. 1431; St. John Hope, Pl. XXIX), and on his tomb in Westminster Abbey (Historical Monuments Commission, Westminster Abbey, Pl. 65, p. 37). Hope conjectures that it may allude to 'the spiritual triumph of St. Katharine over the tyrant Maximian'. Sir Robert Walpole was sixth in descent from Edward Walpole of Houghton and his wife Lucy, daughter and (on the death of her niece Amy Robsart, Countess of Leicester) heir of Sir Terry Robsart, son of Sir John and nephew of Sir Lewis Robsart, both Knights of the Garter.

Plate XXII

100

WILLIAM PITT, EARL OF CHATHAM
Born 1708, died 1778

SHIELD. *Sable a fess chequy argent and azure between three bezants*

CREST. (*On a Peer's helmet*) *On a wreath of the colours a stork proper reposing the dexter foot on an anchor or*

MANTLING. *Gules doubled ermine*

SUPPORTERS. *On the dexter side of his arms a lyon guardant, charged on the breast with a slip of oak fructed proper; and on the sinister a stag proper, attired or, gorged with a collar and chain affixed thereto passing between his forelegs and reflexed over his back sable*

MOTTO. *Benigno numine*

Arms allowed, given, granted, ratified and confirmed by William Camden, Clarenceux, 13 Aug. 1604, to William Pitt of Stepleton, Co. Dorset, great-great-great-uncle of Lord Chatham, '*In a sheild sables a fesse chequie argent and azure betweene three besaunts and for his creast uppon an healme on a wreath or and sables an eagrett in his proper and natural coullours mantled gules doubled silver*'. Crest in lieu of this last granted by Stephen Martin Leake, Garter, 5 Dec. 1761, to the Rt. Hon. William Pitt on his marriage to Hester, Baroness Chatham. Supporters granted to him by the same Garter, 20 Aug. 1766, upon his being created Earl of Chatham.

Plate XXI

101

SIR ISAAC NEWTON

Born 1642, died 1727

Sable two shin bones in saltire argent

Allowed at the Visitation of Lincolnshire, 1634, to Thomas Newton of Gunnerby, nephew of John of Westby, Sir Isaac's great-great-grandfather. A pedigree recorded in the College of Arms by Sir Isaac in 1705 bears his own signature. These Arms are given for 'Newton' in Harl. MS. 6163, fo. 28 (c. 1480-1500; Foster, Two Tudor Books of Arms, p. 172).

Plate XXIII

102

JONATHAN SWIFT, DEAN OF ST. PATRICK'S

Born 1667, died 1745

Sable an anchor in pale or stock azure the stem entwined by a dolphin descending argent

Funeral Entry in the Office of Arms, Dublin, for Godwin Swift of Dublin, (died 7 Dec. 1695), son and heir of Thomas Swift, clerk, of Goodrich, Co. Hereford, and brother of the Dean. The dolphin was perhaps originally a 'swift' or newt.

Plate XXIII

103

HENRY FIELDING

Born 1707, died 1745

Argent on a fess azure three lozenges or
For cadency a mullet within an annulet

Henry Fielding was eldest son of the third son of the fifth son of George Fielding, Earl of Desmond. Dugdale (Antiquities of Warwickshire, 1730, Vol. I, pp. 86-7) states that these Arms are found on seals of the Fieldings of Newnham Paddocks as early as the reign of Edward III, but the entry in Thomas Wriothesley's Roll of Patents (Archaeologia, Vol. 69, p. 91, No. 290) seems to imply that a grant of them was made in the reign of Henry VI.

Plate XXIII

104
HENRY ST. JOHN, VISCOUNT BOLINGBROKE
Born 1678, died 1756

Argent on a chief gules two mullets or
For cadency a crescent (sable) charged with a label of three points (or)

The marks of cadency are shown as in the Patent of 26 July 1712 granting Lord Bolingbroke Supporters upon his being created Viscount. He bore a label because his father was still living, and upon a crescent as descending from Oliver St. John of Lydiard Tregoze (died 1497), second son of Sir Oliver St. John of Bletso, Co. Bedford. Harl. MS. 2169, fo. 25b (The Ancestor, No. 4, p. 248; Foster, Two Tudor Books of Arms, p. 31), gives for 'Sir John Sengone of Walys', probably Sir Oliver's elder son, *Argent on a chief gules two pierced mullets argent.* This is a differenced version of the Arms of the ancient St. Johns of Basing, from whom the St. Johns of Fonmon, Bletso, and Lydiard probably descend, and whose original coat they soon afterwards assumed. Glover's Roll (c. 1245; MS. in the writer's possession) blazons for '. . . *St. Johan, d'argent od chief de gules et deux estoiles d'or en le chief'.*

105
PHILIP DORMER STANHOPE, EARL OF CHESTERFIELD, KNIGHT OF THE GARTER
Born 1694, died 1773

Quarterly ermine and gules

On Lord Chesterfield's Garter Stall Plate. John Stanhope, Bailiff of Newcastle on Tyne and Burgess for the town, who was of this family, bore on his Seal in 1361, *Quarterly, 1 and 4 Ermine, 2 and 3 Four annulets.*

106
ROBERT CLIVE, BARON CLIVE
Born 1725, died 1774

Argent on a fess sable three mullets or

Arms entered for Ambrose Clive of Stych (who signs the Pedigree), great-great-great-grandfather of Lord Clive, at the Visitation of Shropshire 1623.

Plate XXIII

107

CAPTAIN JAMES COOK
Born 1728, died 1779

Azure between two polar stars or a sphere on the plane of the Meridian, North Pole elevated, Circles of latitude for every ten degrees and of longitude for fifteen, shewing the Pacific Ocean between sixty and two hundred and forty west, bounded on one side by America and on the other by Asia and New Holland, in Memory of his having explored and made Discoveries in that Ocean, so very far beyond all former Navigators: His Track thereon marked with red lines.

Granted 3 Sep. 1785 by Isaac Heard, Garter, and Thomas Lock, Clarenceux, on the request of Elizabeth Cook of Mile End, Captain Cook's widow, for a Grant of 'such Armorial Ensigns as may allude to his distinguished character', to be borne by his descendants 'and placed on any Monument or otherwise to his Memory'.

Plate XXIII

108

GEORGE BRYDGES RODNEY, BARON RODNEY
Born 1719, died 1792

Or three eagles displayed purpure

Given for 'Sir Walter Rodeney' in the Powell Roll (c. 1350; No. 271), from whom Lord Rodney was fourteenth in descent, and allowed at the Visitation of Somerset, 1623, to Sir Edward Rodney of Rodney Stoke, Lord Rodney's great-grand-uncle. Willement's Roll gives for 'Monsr. John de Rodneye', *Or three eagles gules*, perhaps a differenced version.

Plate XXIII

109

SIR RICHARD ARKWRIGHT
Born 1732, died 1792

Argent on a mount vert a cotton tree fructed proper and on a chief azure between two bezants an inescocheon of the field charged with a bee volant proper

Granted and exemplified 29 Jan. 1787 by Sir Isaac Heard, Garter, and George Harrison, Norroy, to Sir Richard Arkwright. The bee perhaps stands for industry, the bezants for wealth and the cotton tree for Arkwright's invention.

Plate XXIV

110

EDWARD GIBBON

Born 1737, died 1794

(probably) *Sable a lion rampant argent between three escallops or*

There is some uncertainty as to the proper form of these Arms. Edward Gibbon himself used '*A lyon, rampant, gardant, between three scallop shells, silver on a field azure*', as he tells us in his autobiography (cf. his Seal in the possession of W. J. Hemp, F.S.A., described in The Antiquaries Journal, Vol. XVIII, pp. 406-8, where the Arms and Pedigree are also discussed by the present writer). But this is the Coat of the Gibbons of Rolvenden, of whom was John Gibbon, Bluemantle; and Edward Gibbon was mistaken in thinking that he belonged to this family and that his great-grandfather, Matthew Gibbon, was Bluemantle's brother. Matthew came in fact from Westcliffe, Kent, where his ancestors can be traced back to 1596 (Berry, Kentish Genealogies, pp. 409-11; Hasted, History of Kent, Vol. IV, p. 29; A. W. Gibbons, Gibbons Family Notes, 1884, p. 46). Sir William Segar, Garter 1603-1633, confirmed variations of the same coat to three Kentish families of Gibbon, living at Rolvenden, Bethersden, and Westcliffe. The Pedigree of the latter's senior branch entered at the 1663 Visitation has a note, 'have armes confirmed by Segar Garter', but unfortunately the Arms in question are omitted. Another entry in the College of Arms for 'Gibbon of Westcliffe' is imperfect, giving '. . . a lion rampant [not *guardant*] between 3 escallops', without tinctures. Hasted, however (History of Kent, Vol. IV, p. 29), who may have seen the original Patent, states positively that the coat assigned by Segar to the Gibbons of Westcliffe was, *Sable a lion rampant guardant argent between three escallops or*.

111

HORACE WALPOLE, EARL OF ORFORD

Born 1717, died 1797

Or on a fess between two chevronels sable three cross crosslets of the first
For cadency a mullet

See under his father, Robert Walpole, Earl of Orford (No. 99), whose third son he was (the mullet was of course dropped when he succeeded to the Earldom, but being borne by him for most of his life is here shown).

93

95

96

97

98

101

ROBERT WALPOLE, EARL OF ORFORD,
KNIGHT OF THE GARTER.

WILLIAM PITT,
EARL OF CHATHAM.

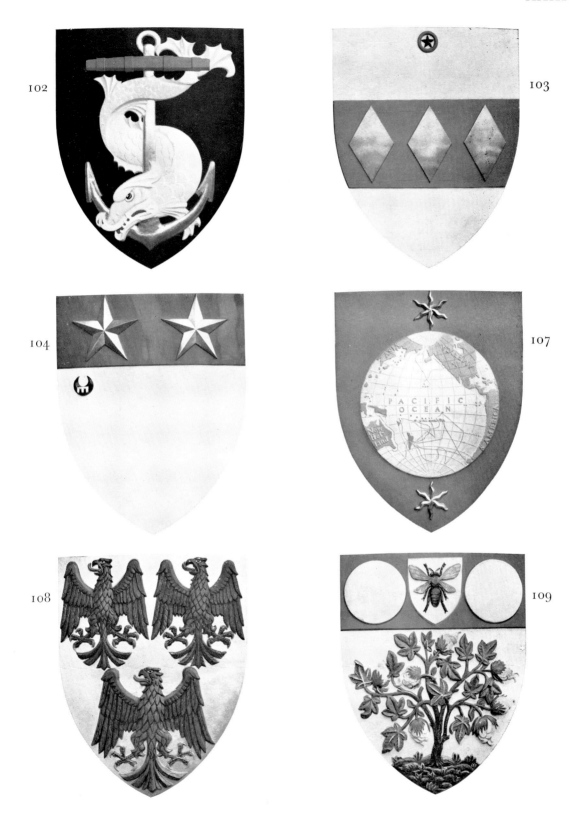

XXIV

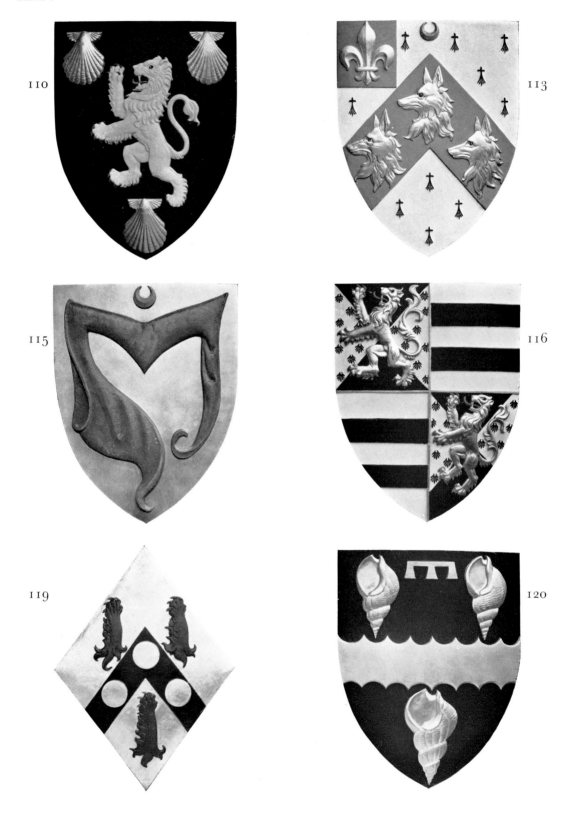

110

113

115

116

119

120

EDMUND BURKE
Born 1729, died 1797

Or a cross gules in the first quarter a lion rampant sable

A certificate of these Arms, as they appear on a tablet to Burke's memory in Beaconsfield Church, Buckinghamshire, was given by Sir John Bernard Burke, Ulster, 15 June 1855. This coat, borne by most Irish families of Burke, is that of the Lords Clanricarde, heirs male of the great Irish house of de Burgh or Bourke after the extinction of their kinsmen the Earls of Ulster, who bore the simple coat, *Or a cross gules*.

Their first known ancestor, William fitz Adelm, Governor of Ireland (died 1204-5), was probably akin to Hubert de Burgh, Earl of Kent (No. 14). It has been suggested (Herald and Genealogist, Vol. IV, pp. 337-40) that the cross of the Earls of Ulster may have been the original de Burgh bearing, since Sir Stephen de Penchester who married Margery, daughter and coheir of John de Burgh, grandson of Hubert, bore *Gules a cross argent*.

However Sir Isaac Heard, Carter, and George Harrison, Clarenceux, exemplified 30 April 1818 to Burke's nephew Thomas William Aston Haviland-Burke arms for Burke *Or a cross gules in the dexter canton a hand couped at the wrist sable.*

Plate XXIV

113
CHARLES JAMES FOX
Born 1749, died 1806

Ermine on a chevron azure three foxes' heads erased or, on a canton of the second a fleur de lys of the third

For cadency a crescent

Granted by Sir Edward Walker, Garter, 30 Oct. 1658, at Brussels, by special command of Charles II to Stephen Fox (Charles James was second son of his son Henry, who was created Lord Holland), 'borne of honest parents at Farley in the County of Wilts', who having 'from his youth been educated in the Royall family and some yeares past by his Majesty's peculiar election haveing ben advanced to the trust and charge of Clerke of his Majesty's Kitchen takeinge likewise care of and ordering the expences of the household in His Majesty's journeyes and residence in these parts hath in the execution thereof behaved himselfe with extraordinary dilligence fidellity prudence and abillity to the great advantage and satisfaction of his Majesty and his service'.

114
WILLIAM PITT
Born 1759, died 1806

Sable a fess chequy argent and azure between three bezants
For cadency a crescent

Pitt was second son of Lord Chatham (No. 100).

Plate XXIV

115

WARREN HASTINGS, GOVERNOR-GENERAL OF INDIA
Born 1732, died 1818

Or a maunch gules; a crescent sable for cadency

These Arms (with the crescent) were allowed to John Hastings of Yelford, Oxfordshire, and Daylesford, Worcestershire (direct ancestor of Warren Hastings), at the Visitation of Oxfordshire in 1634 and to his cousin John Hastings at the Visitation of London in the same year. It may, however, be questioned with what propriety the Arms of Hastings of Daylesford were thus assimilated to those of Hastings, Earl of Pembroke, for the Arms of this family's ancestor, Sir Miles Hastings of Daylesford, are thus given in the Parliamentary Roll under Oxfordshire, '*Sire Miles de Hastynges de or a une fesse de goules en le chef ij moles de goules*'.

Plate XXIV

116

HENRY GRATTAN
Born 1746, died 1820

Quarterly, 1 *and* 4, GRATTAN, *Per saltire sable and ermine a lion rampant or*
2 *and* 3, BRERETON, *Argent two bars sable*

Confirmed by John Hawkins, Ulster, 8 Dec. 1744, to Charles Grattan of Enniskillen, fourth son of the Rev. Patrick Grattan, senior fellow of Trinity College, Dublin, by Grissel, daughter and coheir of Arthur Brereton, fourth son of Edward Brereton of Loughteague, Co. Cavan. Henry was grandson of Henry, eldest son of Patrick. The Grattan Coat is really that confirmed 26 June 1560 by William Hervy, Clarenceux, to Richard Grafton of London, '*Gerondy of foure ermyne and sable over all a lyon rampant golde armed and langyd gules*'.

Plate XXV

117

HORATIO NELSON, VISCOUNT NELSON OF THE NILE,
KNIGHT OF THE BATH
Born 1758, died 1805

SHIELD. *Or a cross flory sable a bend gules surmounted by another engrailed of the
field charged with three bombs fired proper.*
AUGMENTATION. *A chief undulated argent, thereon waves of the sea from which*

90

a palm-tree issuant between a disabled ship on the dexter and a ruinous battery on the sinister all proper
Within the circlet of the Order of the Bath

Two Crests. *Above a Viscount's coronet.*

DEXTER (AUGMENTATION). *On a Naval Crown or, the Chelengk or Plume of Triumph presented to him by the Grand Signior*

SINISTER. *On a Peer's helmet, and wreath of the colours, the stern of a Spanish Man of War proper thereon inscribed 'San Josef'*

SUPPORTERS. *On the dexter, A Sailor armed with a cutlass and a pair of pistols in his belt proper, the exterior hand supporting a staff, thereon hoisted a Commodore's flag Gules, and for augmentation, in the left hand of the sailor a palm branch proper. On the sinister a lion rampant reguardant proper, in his mouth a broken flagstaff, therefrom flowing a Spanish flag, Or and Gules, and for augmentation, a palm branch proper in the paw of the lion with the addition of a tricoloured flag and staff in the mouth of the latter*

MOTTO. *Palmam qui meruit ferat*

Original Arms and sinister Crest granted, exemplified and confirmed 28 Oct. 1797 but Sir Isaac Heard, Garter, and Thomas Lock, Clarenceux, to Sir Horatio Nelson for himself and the other descendants of his father Edmund Nelson, Rector of Burnham Thorpe, Co. Norfolk, representing 'that he is descended by tradition from the family of Nelson registered in the Heralds' Visitation of Lancashire Anno 1664, his family having borne the Arms appertaining to the family so registered, but being unable from the want of family evidences to ascertain his connection with the said family'. Nelson of Fayrehurst at this Visitation bore, *Or a cross patée throughout sable over all a bend gules.* The Arms were granted to Nelson 'as a memorial of his distinguish'd services and merits'. 'San Josef' was 'the name of one of the line of battle-ships taken in the engagement with the Spanish Fleet off Cape St. Vincent on the fourteenth day of February 1797 by his Majesty's Fleet under the command of Sir John Jervis Knight of the Most Honorable Order of the Bath now Earl of Saint Vincent'. Supporters granted to Nelson as a Knight of the Bath 9 Nov. 1797 by Sir Isaac Heard, Garter. Augmentations granted to him as Baron Nelson of the Nile, 20 Dec. 1798, by the same Garter, in virtue of a Royal Warrant of 15 Nov. 1798, signifying that 'beeing desirous of giving a further proof of the sense his Majesty entertains of the great zeal courage and perseverance manifested by him upon divers occasions and particularly of his able and gallant conduct in the glorious and decisive victory obtained over the French fleet near the mouth of the Nile on the first day of August last hath . . . thought fit . . .'

His Pedigree recorded in the College of Arms, showing that his mother was Sir Robert Walpole's great-niece, bears his signature dated 4 Nov. 1797, and somewhat shaky because written with his left hand shortly after he had lost his right arm (Heralds' Commemorative Exhibition 1484-1934, Catalogue, No. 12, Pl. XLVII).

Plate XXV   118

ARTHUR WELLESLEY, DUKE OF WELLINGTON, KNIGHT OF THE GARTER
Born 1769, died 1842

SHIELD. *Quarterly, 1 and 4, WESLEY OR WELLESLEY, Gules a cross argent between five plates saltier ways in each quarter*
>*2 and 3, COLLEY OR COWLEY, Or a lion rampant gules ducally gorged of the field*

AUGMENTATION. *Upon the family Arms of Wellesley and Cowley quarterly and in the chief point of the shield an inescucheon azure charged with the crosses saltire of Saint Andrew and Saint Patrick quarterly per saltire counterchanged argent and gules the latter fimbriated of the second surmounted by the cross of Saint George of the third fimbriated as the saltire, being the Union Badge of the United Kingdom of Great Britain and Ireland without the Imperial Crown*
Within the Garter

CREST. *On a Peer's helmet, within a Duke's coronet, on a wreath of the colours. Out of a ducal coronet or a demi lion rampant holding in his paws a pennant gules one third per pale from the staff argent charged with the cross of Saint George*
For cadency, a mullet on crest and shield

MANTLING. *Gules and argent*

SUPPORTERS. *On either side a lion gules gorged with an Eastern coronet and chained or*

MOTTO. *Virtutis fortuna comes*

The design is based on his Garter Stall Plate. Arms and Crest confirmed to Lord Mornington, the Duke's father, by James McCulloch, Ulster, in 1759. *His* father, Richard Colley, had assumed the name and Arms of Wesley in 1728 on succeeding to the estates of his cousin Garret Wesley of Dangan. The Colley lion is sometimes given with, sometimes without, the coronet round his neck. The Augmentation was exemplified to the Duke by Sir Isaac Heard, Garter, 4 June 1814, in virtue of a Royal Licence of 24 May 1814, superceding a previous Augmentation of a like escocheon of the Union Badge borne in the first quarter of the Wellesley Coat, which was exemplified by the same Garter, 17 Feb. 1813, in virtue of a Royal Warrant of 25 Aug. 1812, signifying 'that His Majesty taking into His Royal Consideration the Glorious and Transcendant Achievements of Arthur Earl of Wellington . . . Commander of His Majesty's Forces in Spain and Portugal . . . and more particularly in the recent brilliant and decisive victory obtained over the French Army by the Troops under his Command near Salamanca on the 22d. day of July last . . . hath thought fit. . . .'

The Union Badge, which is a shield of the Union Flag, imperially crowned, was laid down by Royal Warrant of 1 Jan. 1801, upon the Union with Ireland.

The Supporters were granted to Sir Arthur Wellesley, as a Knight Companion of the Bath, by the same Garter, 23 Jan. 1806.

Plate XXIV

119
JANE AUSTEN *
Born 1775, died 1817

ON A LOZENGE. (probably) *Argent on a chevron between three lions' Gambs erased sable three bezants*

Jane Austen's ancestry has not hitherto been proved beyond her great-great-great-great-grandfather (Berry's Kentish Genealogies, 1830, p. 127), John Austen of Horsmonden, who was buried there 5 March 1620. A brass shield of Arms, *Three roundels on a chevron between three lions' gambs erased*, remains on the tomb of his wife Joan, buried there 16 Dec. 1604 (Hasted, History of Kent, 1782, Vol. II, p. 387). This Coat, with tinctures as above, was allowed at the 1574 Visitation of Kent to James Astyn of Chevening, and Stephen Astyn (or Austen) of Yalding, the next parish to Horsmonden. Austen is a common name in Kent, and similar Arms are recorded for three Kentish families of the name. The use of this particular coat by John, so near in place and time to the Visitation family, decidedly suggests relationship. Such other evidence as I have found tends to confirm this. John Awsten of Horsmonden, in a deposition at Canterbury (Register of Depositions, Vol. 14, p. 80) made in 1591-2, states that he was then aged 32 and was born at Goudhurst. The Horsmonden Register shows no John Austen other than Jane's ancestor to whom this deposition could belong. The Goudhurst Register shows only one entry that will fit John's date of birth as stated above—the baptism, namely, of an unnamed son of Robert Austen 26 April 1560. A consecutive series of his children's baptisms shows that this Robert was of Horsmonden, where he was buried in 1603, and that among them was a son Stephen, baptized at Goudhurst in 1561. Now the Visitation pedigree shows that Stephen Austen of Yalding had a son Robert by his second marriage with Dorothy Peckham, and I conjecture that this Robert is identical with the father of John of Horsmonden. The dates fit, for Margaret, Stephen's first wife, was living in 1522 when his father, William Astyn of Yalding, made his Will (P.C.C. 25 Maynwaryng), and his second marriage to Dorothy Peckham must have taken place not long after, for by 1574 James of Chevening, a son of this marriage, was himself married and had issue. The occurrence of Stephen as the name of Robert's son supports the identification.

Plate XXVI

120
PERCY BYSSHE SHELLEY
Born 1792, died 1822

Sable a fess engrailed between three whelk shells or, a label for cadency

Shown on the brass of John Shelley, 1526, at Clapham, Sussex; allowed at the Visitation of Sussex 1634; a canting Coat.

Plate XXVI

121

GEORGE GORDON BYRON, BARON BYRON
Born 1788, died 1824

Argent three bendlets enhanced gules

The 'enhancement' of the bends seems to date only from the late fifteenth century, the first occurrence I have found being in Ballard's Book (c. 1480-1500; Coll. Arm. MS. M.3, fo. 38), for 'Nicholas Berron of Claiton'. The Parliamentary Roll (c. 1310) blazons '*Sire James Byroun de argent a iij bendes de goules*', and the same form is found as late as Henry VI's reign in Harl. MS. 2169, fo. 19 (The Ancestor, No. 4, p. 236; pace Foster, Two Tudor Books of Arms, p. 21). The first Lord Byron's great-grandfather, John Byron of Clayton, Lancashire, was a bastard, being, as the 1567 Visitation of Lancashire puts it, 'sonne and heire by deade of gifte to Sir John Byron knight', and accordingly bore his paternal Arms within a border azure. This mark of bastardy seems, however, to have been dropped by the first Lord Byron (Coll. Arm. MS. Walker's Nobility, p. 173). Byron himself, by Royal Warrant of 27 Feb. and exemplification by Sir Isaac Heard, Garter, dated 1 March 1822, assumed the surname and Arms of Noel (being those of his wife) in lieu of those of Byron—the Arms, *Or fretty gules a canton ermine, with a quartrefoil sable for distinction.*

Plate XXVI

122

SIR WALTER SCOTT, BARONET
Born 1771, died 1832

Quarterly, 1 *and* 4, SCOTT, *Or two mullets in chief and a crescent in base azure within an orle of the second*
2 *and* 3, HALIBURTON, *Or on a bend azure three mascles of the first in the sinister chief point a buckle of the second*
The Baronet's Badge, an inescutcheon argent, charged with a sinister hand gules

Matriculated in Lyon Register 7 March 1820, the first quarter being a differenced version of the Arms matriculated 1672-7 by 'George Scot of Boonraw Representer of the old familie of Sintoune', '*Or two mollets in chiefe and ane crescent in base azur*'. Sir Walter's great-grandfather was a cadet of Scott of Raeburn, and grandson of a cadet of Scott of Harden, whose senior line represented Scott of Sinton after the extinction of Boonraw. Sinton was in turn an old cadet of Buccleuch, and William of Harden in 1540 sealed with the Arms of

94

Buccleuch, *On a bend a crescent between two mullets* (Laing, Scottish Seals, 1866, No. 884). The earliest form of the Buccleuch Coat, *On a bend a mullet and two crescents and in sinister chief a mullet*, appears on the Seal of Robert, lord of Buccleuch, in 1415 (William Fraser, The Scotts of Buccleuch, 1878, Vol. I, p. 529), and the same bearing appears on that of William of Sinton in 1550 (ib. p. 534). Sir Walter mistakenly thought that the bend was for Murdieston, and not borne by Sinton and Harden, as branching from Buccleuch prior to the Murdieston match (ib. p. 528); hence the absence of the bend from his own matriculation. Sir Walter's grandmother was heiress of Haliburton of Newmains, who had matriculated, 1672-7, *Or on a bend azur three mascles in the sinister canton a buckle of the first*, a differenced version of the Coat of Haliburton of Dirleton, which appears c. 1340 in the Balliol Roll (Coll. Arm. MS. Vincent 164, fo. 110b) for 'Sr. de Halyberton' as, *Argent on a bend gules three mascles or*, and c. 1370 in the Armorial de Gelre (R.R. Stoddart, Scottish Arms, 1881, Vol. I, Pl. C) for 'Gauthier Haliburton', as, *Or on a bend azure three mascles argent*.

Plate XXVI

123
WILLIAM WILBERFORCE
Born 1759, died 1833

Argent an eagle displayed sable beaked and legged gules

Harl. MS. 2169, fo. 25 (temp. Henry VI; The Ancestor, No. 4, p. 246; Foster, Two Tudor Books of Arms, p. 30) gives this Coat for 'Rychard Wylbyrforse of Yorkchyre'. Entered for Wilberfosse of Wilberfosse at the Visitations of Yorkshire in 1584 and 1665. William was seventh in descent from Thomas of Beverley, younger brother of Roger Wilberfosse of Wilberfosse who signed the Pedigree in 1584.

Plate XXVI

124
SAMUEL TAYLOR COLERIDGE
Born 1772, died 1834

Argent on a mount in base vert an otter statant proper on a chief gules a dove close proper between two crosses patée fitchée or
An annulet for cadency

Granted 14 May 1824 by Sir George Nayler, Garter, and Ralph Bigland, Clarenceux, to William Hart Coleridge (then about to be appointed Bishop of Barbadoes) for himself and the other descendants of his late grandfather John Coleridge, Vicar of Ottery St. Mary, Co. Devon. Samuel Taylor was fifth surviving son of John. The otter presumably alludes to Ottery St. Mary; the dove and crosses would become a colonial bishop.

Plate XXVI

125

GEORGE STEPHENSON
Born 1781, died 1848

Argent a cheveron between two fleurs-de-lis in chief and a cross fleurettée in base gules a chief azure thereon three mullets of the first

Granted and confirmed 21 Nov. 1838 by Sir William Woods, Garter, Edmund Lodge, Clarenceux, and Joseph Hawker, Norroy, to Robert Stephenson, son of George, for himself, his father and their descendants.

Plate XXVI

126

SIR ROBERT PEEL, BARONET
Born 1788, died 1850

Argent three sheaves of as many arrows two and one proper banded gules, on a chief azure a bee volant or
In chief the Baronet's Badge, an inescutcheon argent charged with a sinister hand gules

Granted and exemplified 7 March 1792 by Sir Isaac Heard, Garter, and George Harrison, Norroy, to Robert Peel of Oswaldtwissle, Lancashire, and Manchester (grandfather of Sir Robert), for himself and the other descendants of his father William Peel.

Plate XXVII

127

THOMAS BABINGTON MACAULAY, BARON
MACAULAY OF ROTHLEY
Born 1800, died 1859

Gules two arrows saltirewise points downward argent surmounted by as many barrulets compony or and azure between two buckles in pale of the third all within a bordure engrailed also of the third

Granted and confirmed 30 Oct. 1857 by Sir Charles George Young, Garter, to Lord Macaulay, for himself and the other descendants of his father Zachary Macaulay.

1758   1805
HORATIO NELSON, VISCOUNT NELSON,
KNIGHT OF THE BATH

1769   1852
ARTHUR WELLESLEY, DUKE OF WELLINGTON
KNIGHT OF THE GARTER.

121

122

123

124

125

126

Plate XXVII

128

WILLIAM MAKEPEACE THACKERAY
Born 1811, died 1863

Vert two garbs or, in base an arrow argent, on a chief purpure, a cherub's head proper between the like number of estoiles of the third
A mullet for cadency

Given, granted, ratified and confirmed, 17 Feb. 1755, by Stephen Martin Leake, Garter, and Charles Townley, Clarenceux, to Thomas Thackeray, D.D., Archdeacon of Surrey. William Makepeace was only son of Richmond, eldest son of William Makepeace, the third son of Thomas to leave issue.

129

HENRY JOHN TEMPLE, VISCOUNT PALMERSTON
Born 1784, died 1865

Quarterly, 1 and 4, Or an eagle displayed sable
 2 and 3, Argent two bars sable each charged with three mullets or

Certified and declared by Sir John Bernard Burke, Ulster, 23 Nov. 1869, to be Lord Palmerston's Arms. Lord Palmerston traced descent from Anthony, younger son of Peter Temple of Burton Dassett. The latter was granted Arms by Sir Gilbert Dethick, 8 Feb. 1569, '*The field argent, on a cheveron sable betweene 3 crescentes gueules 5 martlets of the first*'. A different coat, however, *Sable a chevron ermine between three martlets argent,* was confirmed to him by Robert Cooke, Clarenceux, 10 Nov. 1576, and it is this that appears in the Visitations of Buckinghamshire 1575 and Leicestershire 1619. At the 1634 Visitation of Buckinghamshire, however, the Coat given above in the second and third quarters was allowed to Sir Thomas Temple of Stowe, Baronet, grandson of Peter of Burton Dassett, and to his son Sir Peter; and a later copy in the College of Arms (MS. Philipot 29, fo. 61b) has a note: 'This coate and creast was here set down by the desire of Sr Peter Temple Kt & Baronet who affirmed it to be his auntient Creast, & now beareth it in this manner. Jo: Withy. Ao. 1650'. These arms, no doubt, allude to the name. The notion of 'temple haunting martlets' derives from Psalm 84, verse 4. The Coat in the first and fourth quarters appears, quartered as above, in the 1662 Visitation of Surrey, being allowed to Sir Purbeck Temple of Edgecombe, nephew of Sir Peter. It is (though not so named there) the fabulous coat attributed to Leofric, Earl of Mercia (The Rows Roll, ed. William Courthope, 1859, No. 27), from whom a no less fabulous descent has sometimes been claimed for the Temples (J. H. Round, Peerage and Family History, 1901, p. 45).

Plate XXVII

130

BENJAMIN DISRAELI, EARL OF BEACONSFIELD
Born 1804, died 1881

Per saltire gules and argent a tower triple towered in chief proper two lions rampant in fess sable and an eagle displayed in base or

Granted and confirmed 16 Oct. 1876 by Sir Albert William Woods, Garter, to Lord Beaconsfield, for himself and the other descendants of his father Isaac Disraeli.

131

CHARLES ROBERT DARWIN
Born 1809, died 1882

Argent on a bend gules cottised vert, between two mullets each within an annulet gules three escallops or

Granted and assigned 6 March 1890 (after Charles Darwin's death) by Sir Albert William Woods, Garter, Walter Aston Blount, Clarenceux, and George Edward Cokayne, Norroy, to Reginald Darwin of Fern, Co. Derby, for himself and the other descendants of his father, Sir Francis Sacheverel Darwin, and his uncle Robert Waring Darwin (father of Charles); the Arms previously borne by the family—*Argent on a bend gules cottised vert three escallops or*— not being duly registered in the College of Arms.

Plate XXVII

132

ANTHONY ASHLEY COOPER, EARL OF SHAFTESBURY
Born 1801, died 1885

Quarterly, 1 *and* 4, *for* Ashley, *Argent three oxen statant sable armed and unguled*
or
2 *and* 3, Cooper, *Gules a bend engrailed between six lions rampant or*

The Coat borne for Ashley seems actually to be the canting one of Brayboef (ox=boeuf). The manor of Cranborne in Wonston, Hampshire (Victoria County History, Hampshire, Vol. III, p. 459) passed through heiresses from the Brayboef family to Egidia (died 1476), daughter of Sir John Hamelyn and wife of Robert Ashley. The paternal Coat of Ashley was, *Azure a cinquefoil and bordure engrailed ermine*, but for this the Brayboef Coat was sometimes (as in the 1530 Visitation of Dorset), though by no means always, substituted. Lord Shaftesbury descends in the male line from John Cooper or Cowper of Stanton Drew, Somerset, to whom Sir William Dethick, Garter, on the 23rd of April 1593, confirmed and exemplified the Arms '*Gules a bend engrayled betweene six lyons rampants gould armed and langued azure*'. This John's son married the Ashley heiress, and their son, who was created in 1661 Lord Ashley and in 1672 Earl of Shaftesbury, placed Ashley (or Brayboef) in the first quarter and his paternal Coat of Cooper in the second in or before the latter year.

133
CHARLES STEWART PARNELL
Born 1846, died 1891

Gules two cheveronels in chief three escallops argent
A crescent on a crescent for cadency

Confirmed and exemplified 10 March 1842 by Sir William Woods, Garter, to Henry Brooke Parnell, Baron Congleton, for himself and other descendants of his late father Sir John Parnell, Baronet. Charles Stewart was second surviving son of John Henry Parnell of Avondale, only son of William Parnell-Hayes, second surviving son of Sir John Parnell.

Plate XXVII

134
ALFRED TENNYSON, BARON TENNYSON
Born 1809, died 1892

Gules on a bend nebuly or between three leopards' faces jessant-de-lis of the last, a wreath of laurel proper

Granted and comfirmed 2 Feb. 1884 by Sir Albert William Woods, Garter, to Lord Tennyson for himself and the other descendants of his father the late George Clayton Tennyson, Rector of Somersby, Lincolnshire. The laurel wreath befits a poet laureate. Tennyson's mother was Elizabeth daughter of the Rev. Stephen Fytche, vicar of Louth, who claimed descent from the family of Fitch of Lindsell, to whom arms *Vert a chevron between three leopards' faces or* were allowed at the Visitation of Essex 1570. Hence, probably, the leopards' faces in Tennyson's coat. It is likely that the Fitch arms in turn derive from those of Wentworth (see No. 77) of whom a branch were settled at Nettlested in Suffolk and later at several places in Essex.

Plate XXVII

135

WILLIAM MORRIS *
Born 1834, died 1896

Azure a horse's head erased argent between three horse shoes or

Granted and assigned 15 April 1843 by Sir Charles George Young, Garter, and Joseph Hawker, Clarenceux, to William Morris of Woodford Hall, Essex (father of William Morris).

Plate XXVIII

136

WILLIAM EWART GLADSTONE
Born 1809, died 1898

Argent a savage's head affronté distilling drops of blood and wreathed about the temples with holly proper within an orle fleury gules the whole within eight martlets in orle sable.
A martlet for cadency

Granted and confirmed 1 July 1846 by Sir Charles George Young, Garter, and James Pulman, Norroy, to John Gladstone of Fasque and Balfour, Co. Kincardine, for himself and the other descendants of his late father Thomas Gladstones. John Gladstone had dropped the final 's' by Royal Licence dated 10 Feb. 1835, and was created a Baronet 18 July 1846 Mr. Gladstone was his fourth son.

137

JOHN RUSKIN
Born 1819, died 1900

Sable on a cheveron between six spear heads argent three cross crosslets fitchée gules

Granted and confirmed 10 Jan. 1835 by Sir Ralph Bigland, Garter, and Sir William Woods, Clarenceux, to John James Ruskin of the City of London and Herne Hill, Surrey, merchant (father of John).

Plate XXVIII

138

CECIL JOHN RHODES
Born 1853, died 1902

Argent within two bendlets a lion passant gules between two thistles stalked and leaved proper
For cadency, a mullet

A posthumous grant of Arms, made 8 Jan. 1913, by Sir Alfred Scott Scott-Gatty, Garter, and William Henry Weldon, Clarenceux, to Arthur Montagu Rhodes, brother of Cecil, for himself and the other descendants of his late father, the Rev. Francis William Rhodes, Vicar of Bishops Stortford, Hertfordshire.

Plate XXVIII

139

WILLIAM THOMSON, BARON KELVIN OF LARGS
Born 1824, died 1907

Argent a stag's head cabossed gules, on a chief azure a thunderbolt proper winged or between two spur revels of the first

Granted by Sir James Balfour Paul, Lyon, 1892 (Sir James Balfour Paul, Ordinary of Scottish Arms, 1903, No. 3370).

Plate XXVIII

140

JOSEPH LISTER, BARON LISTER
Born 1827, died 1912

Ermine on a fess invected sable three mullets of six points argent in chief a staff erect entwined by a serpent proper

Granted 16 Feb. 1884 by Sir Albert William Woods, Garter, and Walter Aston Blount, Clarenceux, to Joseph Lister and the other descendants of his father Joseph Jackson Lister, 'Her Majesty having been graciously pleased to signify Her Royal intention of advancing him to the dignity of a Baronet'. The Arms are based on those of Lister of Midhope (Visitation of Yorkshire 1584-5), *Ermine on a fess sable three mullets or*. The 'staff' is the 'Rod of Aesculapius'.

Plate XXVIII

141

HORATIO HERBERT KITCHENER, EARL KITCHENER OF KHARTOUM
Born 1850, died 1916

Gules a chevron argent surmounted by another azure between three bustards proper in the centre chief point a bezant;
surmounted by the first Augmentation,
A pile or thereon two flag staves saltirewise flowing to the dexter the Union Flag of Great Britain and Ireland and to the sinister a representation of the Egyptian Flag all proper enfiled by a Mural Crown Gules the rim inscribed KHARTOUM *in letters of gold;*
and for the second Augmentation,
A chief argent thereon a pale gules charged with a lion passant guardant or between on the dexter side an eagle displayed sable and on the sinister on a mount vert an orange tree fructed proper

Substantive Coat granted 28 Jan. 1899 by Sir Albert William Woods, Garter, and George Edward Cokayne, Clarenceux, to Francis Elliott Kitchener (first cousin of Lord Kitchener) for himself and the other descendants of his father and uncles. First Augmentation exemplified 7 April 1900 by Sir A. W. Woods, Garter, in virtue of a Royal Warrant dated 26 May 1899, to Horatio Herbert, Baron Kitchener of Khartoum, 'as a lasting memorial of the conspicuous talent and ability displayed by him on divers important occasions during the recent expedition to Omdurman, which terminated in the recapture of Khartoum', for himself and his descendants. Second Augmentation granted and exemplified 8 July 1904 by Alfred Scott Scott-Gatty, Garter, in virtue of a Royal Warrant dated 15 Sept. 1903, to Viscount Kitchener of Khartoum and of the Vaal, 'lately Commander-in-Chief of the Forces in South Africa', for himself and his descendants.

Plate XXVIII   142

ERNEST RUTHERFORD, BARON RUTHERFORD OF NELSON, MEMBER OF THE ORDER OF MERIT
Born 1871, died 1937

Per saltire arched gules and or two inescutcheons voided of the first in fesse within each a martlet sable

Granted to Lord Rutherford 14 Oct. 1931 by Sir Gerald Woods Wollaston, Garter.

GLOSSARY AND SUBJECT INDEX

Heraldic terms are as a rule more easily understood through pictures than explanations. In this glossary (which includes only terms found in the book) definitions have, therefore, been kept to a minimum, their place being taken, where possible, by references to the plates in which examples occur. Arabic numerals (1, 2) refer to the shield and note numbers (those in brackets being of incidental references made in the body of the notes), large Roman (I, II) to the plates and small Roman (i, ii) to the pages of the introduction. The century dates (13c., 14c.) attached to some of the more important entries are those of the earliest occurrence known to the writer of the term or charge in question. They are, however, based only upon general impressions, not exhaustive analysis, and no finality whatever is claimed for them.

ACHIEVEMENT of arms. 16c. Shield with external ornaments. 'Hatchment' is a contraction.

AESCULAPIUS' ROD. XXVIII 140. A staff encircled by a serpent occurs in classical times as an attribute of Aesculapius, and hence is used as an emblem of medicine. See the Antiquary, New Series, II, 1915, pp. 51, 417-8, S.D. Clippingdale, 'Heraldry and Medicine', and Journal of the Michigan State Medical Society, March 1937, H.L. Arnold, 'Serpent-emblems of Medicine'.

ANCHOR. 16c., XXII 100, XXIII 102.

ANNULET. 13c. 'faux rondelett' (see false and roundel), 14c. anel (Latin, annulus), a ring, XII 49, XVI 65, 131. As the cadency mark of a fifth son (83), XXIII 103, XXVI 124.

ANTELOPE. XXII 99 (this is the antelope of nature, not the purely heraldic antelope found as a royal badge in the fifteenth century).

ARCHED. 18 or 19c., XXVIII 142.

ARCHIEPISCOPAL STAFF OF CROSS. XII 51, XIV 63, XVII 71, 88. Its use was allowed to all archbishops by Pope Gregory IX.

ARGENT. 12c. Silver or white.

ARMED. 16c. XX 89, XXVII 132, having teeth, claws, horns, beak or the like of such a tincture.

ARROW. XXVI 126, XXVII 127 and 128.

ATTIRED. 16c. XXII 99 and 100, having the attires, i.e. the antlers (the head attire) of such a tincture.

AUGMENTATION. p. xxxiii, XVI 70, XVII 74, XXV 117 and 118, XXVIII 141.

AZURE. 12 or 13c. Blue (deriving through Arabic from a Persian root found also in Lapis *lazuli*).

BADGE. 14 or 15c., pp. xvi-xvii (28), XI 46; BARONETS' BADGE, XXVI 122 and 126, James I by letters patent dated 28 May 1612 granted 'that the Baronets, and their descendants shall, and may beare, either in a Canton in theire coate of Armes, or, in an Inscutchion, at their election, the Armes of Ulster, that is, in a field Argent, a hand Geules, or a bloudy hand'; UNION BADGE, XXV 118.

BANDED. XXVI 126, tied with a band of such a tincture.

BANNER. XIX 82. A rectangular flag of arms.

BANNERET. A knight entitled to lead his vassals into battle under his own banner. When a knight was made a banneret his pennon (q.v.) was made into a banner by cutting off its tail.

BAR. 13c., XXIV 116, 129. One of two or more horizontal bands (narrower than a fess).

BARBED. 16c., IX 44, XIV 63, XVI 69, XX 90; of a rose, having the barbs (i.e. the five leaves of the calyx) of such a tincture.

BARRULET. 16c., XXVII 127, a narrow bar.

BARRY, barre. 13c., VII 33, XVI 65, a field divided into a number of bars (in modern heraldry always an even number, which is specified, as 'barry of six'). See also Burelly.

103

BASE. The lowest part of the shield. In base, XXVI 122 and 124 and 125, XXVII 128 and 130.

BASTARDY, marks of. Before the late fourteenth century (and in many instances later) no one difference (q.v.) was specially reserved for bastards, their arms being varied from the principal arms of their house neither more nor less than those of legitimate younger sons, cf. XXVI 121. At that time however a fashion began to come in for royal bastards to charge their father's arms on a bend, fess or the like, cf. (52). In modern times the baston and certain borders have been used for this purpose.

BATH, circlet of the Order of the, XXV 117; the practice of thus encircling the arms of Knights of the Bath (by analogy with the Garter q.v.) seems to date only from the revival of the Order in 1725.

BATTERY. XXV 117.

BEAR. XI 46.

BEE. XXIII 109, XXVI 126, probably as an emblem of industry.

BEND, bende, 13c., IV 21, VII 31, IX 42, XI 46, XII 54, XIII 58, XV 64, XVII 78, (XX 80), XXI 96, XXV 117, XXVI 122, XXVII 130 and 132 and 134, diagonal *band* from dexter chief to sinister base (a bend sinister runs from sinister chief to dexter base). In bend, XX 80, disposed in this direction.

BENDLET. 16c., XIX 82, XXVI 121, XXVIII 138, a narrow bend.

BEZANT, besant. 13c., XVII 74, XXII 100, XXIII 109, 114, XXIV 119, XXVIII 141; a roundel or (from the bezant or gold coin of Byzantium).

BEZANTY, besante. 13c., III 15, powdered with bezants.

BILLET, p. xviii, a rectangular figure or block.

BLAZON, pp. xvii-xix, a technical description (French, blason, painted heraldic shield).

BLOOD, drops of. XXVIII 136.

BOAR'S HEAD. XVI 62.

BOMB. XXV 117.

BONE. XXI 101.

BORDURE, border. 13c., II 6, III 15, VIII 39, XII 52 and 54, 53, XIII 57 and 61, XVI 66, XIX 82, XXVIII 127.

BUCKLE. XXVI 122, XXVII 127.

BULL. XI 46. Bull's head. XX 86.

BURELLY, burele. 13c., but not in modern heraldry, VII 30. Barry of a large number.

BUSTARD. XXVIII 141.

CABOSSED, caboshed. 16c., XXVIII 139, of a beast's head, shown full face and without neck. To caboche is to cut off the head (French 'caboche', from Italian 'capocchia', diminutive of 'capo', from Latin 'caput') of a deer close behind the horns.

CADENCY MARKS. p. xxxii, small charges added to a coat to distinguish cadets from the head of their house. Spelman (Aspilogia, 1654, p. 140) attributet their invention to Sir John Writhe, Garter King of Arms 1478-1504. They are given in Gerard Legh's 'Accedens of Armory', 1562. They are (1) The Label, q.v., for an eldest son in his father's lifetime; (2) Crescent, q.v., for a second son; (3) Mullet, q.v., for a third son; (4) Martlet, q.v., for a fourth son; (5) Annulet, q.v., for a fifth son; (6) Fleur de lys, for a sixth son; (7) Rose, for a seventh son; (8) Cross moline, for an eighth son; (9) Double Quatrefoil, ninth son. Cadency marks were often charged on crests as well as shields, XXV 118, and, for younger sons of younger sons or branches, upon one another, XXIII 103 and 104, 133.

CANTING arms, p. xxxii.

CANTON, cauntel. 13c., XVII 74, XIX 82, XXIV 113; a rectangular corner of the shield in dexter chief, in early times filling a whole quarter, but later smaller.

CARDINAL'S HAT. XIV 63.

CASTLE. IX 47.

CATHERINE WHEEL. XXII 99, the instrument of St. Catherine's martyrdom.

CHAIN. XXII 99 and 100, XXV 118.

CHANGE OF ARMS. (23), (59).

CHARGE. Anything borne on a coat of arms.

CHARGED. XXII 100, XXIII 109, XXV 117, XXVI 122; having upon it a charge.

CHELENGK. XXV 117.

CHEQUY, checky. escheque, echiqueté, 13c., IV 22, XI 46, XII 49, XXII 99 and 100, 114; divided like a chessboard into squares of alternate tincture.

CHERUB'S HEAD. XXVII 128.

CHESS ROOK, rok. 13c., XV 64, a castle in chess.

CHEVRON, cheveron. 13c., II 4, 12, IV 16 and 25, 20, VIII 36 and 37, 40, IX 44, XI 46, XII 51 and 55, XIII 57 and 59, XV 64, XVI 62 and 65 and 67, XVII 71, 85, 88, XX 89, 92, 94, XXI 98, XXII 99, 111, XXIV 113 and 119, XXVI 125, 133, 137, XXVIII 141; a figure like two rafters meeting (French, cheveron, rafter).

CHEVRONEL, cheveronel, chevernel. 16c., XXII 99, 111, 133, a narrow chevron.

CHIEF. 13c., II 5, V 27, VII 32 and 33, XIII 60, XIV 63, XVI 66, 83, XX 90, 91, XXI 98, XXIII 104 and 109, XXV 117, XXVI 124 and 125 and 126, XXVII 128, XXVIII 139 and 141. The upper part of the shield cut off by a horizontal line. In chief, XII 49, XVII 74, 77, XXI 95, XXVI 122 and 125 and 126, XXVII 130, 133, XXVIII 140. Chief point XXV 118, (sinister) XXVI 122, (centre) XXVIII 141.

CINQUEFOIL. 13c., p. xviii, III 10, XV 64, and pierced XII 51, XVII 71. A conventional form or flower of five leaves.

CLARENCEUX KING OF ARMS. p. xxi. King of Arms of England South of the Trent. The title was instituted about 1420 perhaps in compliment to Thomas Duke of Clarence, a benefactor of the heralds, the same jurisdiction having previously been held (so Anstis conjectures) by Leicester King of Arms. (Roy d'Armes des Clarenceux, King of Arms of the Clarenceux, i.e. the people of Clarence, i.e. the domain of Clare, by analogy with Norroy, q.v.).

CLOSE. XXVI 124, with wings closed.

COAT OF ARMS. p. xvi, V 27, VI 28, X 45.

COLLAR. XXII 99 and 100.

COLLATERAL ADOPTION of arms, p. xxxi, (3), (4), (5), (12), (22), (33), (39).

COLOURS. 15c., p. xvii, the non-metallic tinctures, viz. gules, azure, sable, vert, purpure.

COMPONY. 16c., Latinization of Gobony, q.v., through mistaken derivation from Latin componere, to put together.

CONGER. IX 48.

CORNER. 13c., but not in modern heraldry, (18), VII 33.

CORNISH CHOUGH. XIV 63.

CORONET. Coronets were worn by Dukes to mark their dignity in Edward III's reign (p. xvi and cf. XI 46), but the use of different patterns to mark the different ranks of peers above the barons came in under Elizabeth. Dukes' coronets, XIX 82, XXV 118, have 8 strawberry leaves; Marquesses' 4 strawberry leaves and 4 pearls; Earls', XXII 99, 8 pearls and 8 small strawberry leaves; Viscounts', XXV 117, 16 pearls. Barons had none until Charles II by Royal Warrant of 7 Aug. 1661 granted them coronets of 4 pearls. The so-called 'Ducal coronet', XXV 118, often found in commoners' crests is simply a crest coronet, older than and having no connection with the use of such a pattern by Dukes. The Eastern coronet, XXV 118, is a modern variety not infrequently granted to persons of eastern connections or services. See also Crown.

COTISE. 13c., IV 21, XIII 58, XV 64, 131; one of two bendlets borne on either side (French côte, from Latin costa, rib) of a bend. Cotised, Cotisee, 13c., of a bend, having cotises.

COTTON TREE. XXIII 109.

COUNTERCHANGED. 16c. III 13, IX 42, X 45, 84, XXV 118, said of charges upon a field divided between two tinctures, when the charges upon each tincture are of the other. The usual mediaeval blazon is 'de l'un en l'autre', or the like.

COUPED. 16c. (but 'recoupy', c. 1390), IX 48, XX 86; cut short by a straight line.

CRESCENT, croissant. 13c., 91, XXVI 122; as the cadency mark of a second son, 73, 83, XXI 96, XXIII 104, XXIV 113 and 115, 114, 133.

H

CREST. p. xvi; (in actual use) v 27, vi 28, x 45, xi 46; (in achievements of arms), xv 64, xviii 81, xix 82, xxii 99 and 100, xxv 117 and 118. The modelled crest is rare before the fourteenth century though one appears as early as 1197 on the seal of Baldwin of Flanders, Emperor of Constantinople. Devices painted on fan shaped metal crests (as in 1 2) occur occasionally in the thirteenth century. While devices painted on the helmet itself go back to the twelfth century, the lion painted on Geoffrey of Anjou's cap in the enamel at Le Mans, (9), being the prototype.

CROSS. 12c., xiv 63, xviii 81, xix 82, 112, xxv 118. The earliest varieties of cross are the Crosses Paty, Furché, Fleureté, Crosslet and Saltire, q.v. Later come the Flory, Formy, Moline, Patonce and other varieties. The Cross of St. George (xviii 81, xxv 118) is Gules upon argent, while those of St. Andrew (xviii 81, xxv 118) and St. Patrick (xxv 118) are Saltires Argent upon azure and Gules upon argent respectively. See also Archiepiscopal and Legatine Cross.

CROSSLET, cross crosslet, croiselette. 13c., viii 37, xi 46, xxi 98, xxii 99, 111. At first simply a small cross of no fixed shape, but in the fourteenth century definitely associated with the type with crossed arms. Before the sixteenth century the ends were rounded, viii 37, xi 46, but later square.

CROWN. viii 39; upon crowned lions, iii 15, iv 18, 19, v 27, vi 28; Imperial crown, xviii 81, crown of the Kings of England; the arched form dates from the fifteenth century, the name Imperial probably from James I, 'Emperor of Great Britain', or Henry VIII. Mural Crown, 17c., xxviii 141, often granted to distinguished soldiers; based on the Roman custom of crowning the soldier who first climbed the walls of a besieged town. Naval Crown, 17c., xxv 118, often given to distinguished sailors, from a similar Roman custom.

CUTLASS. xxv 117.

DANCE. 13c., p. xv. A zigzag fess or bar.

DEXTER. c. 1390 (Johannes de Bado Aureo, ed. Bysshe 1654, p. 44). The wearer's right side of a shield, that is the spectator's left, xii 49, xv 64, 88, xxii 99, xxv 117, xxviii 141; later for right in general, xix 82, xxii 100.

DIFFERENCING. p. xxxii, (2), (5), (6), (17), (19), vi 28, vii 30, viii 36, ix 41 and 43, xii 50 and 52, 53, xiii 61, (77), (104), (108), (110), (122). In mediaeval heraldry, making small alterations to a coat to distinguish different members or branches of a family from one another.

DIMIDIATION, p. xix.

DISPLAYED, espanie, explanata (Johannes de Bado Aureo). 14c., of an eagle (q.v.), spread out. In mediaeval heraldry eagles are always shown in this manner.

DISPOSITION OF CHARGES. When doubtful, explained by such phrases as 'points downward', 'two and one'; 'three, two and one', 'in saltire', 'in chief', 'in fess', q.v.

DOLPHIN. xvi 66, xxiii 102.

DOVE. xxvi 124.

DRAGON. x 45, xiv 63, xviii 81. In modern heraldry this name is limited to the four legged variety, the two legged are called Wyvern, q.v.

EAGLE. vii 29, xi 46, 84, xx 87, xxiii 108, xxvi 123, 129, xxvii 130, xxviii 141. Double headed eagle, xxi 93.

EARS OF BARLEY. xvi 66.

EEL SPEAR. xvi 66.

EMBOWED. 16c., xvi 66, bent.

ENDENTE, see Indented.

ENFILED. 16c., xxviii 131, threaded.

ENGRAILED, engrele. 13c., in mediaeval heraldry a synonym for indented (q.v.), either name being applicable to either of the forms denoted in modern heraldry by the two names (perhaps from French 'grêle', hail, as though 'pitted by hailstones'), (8), viii 34, (43), (80). In modern heraldry, notched with a continuous succession of concavities, xii 54, xiii 56 and 57 and 58, xiv 63, xvi 66 and 67, xx 79, xxv 117, xxiv 120, xxvii 127 and 132.

ENHANCED. XXVI 121. Raised above the normal position.

ERADICATED. XV 64, XIX 82. Uprooted.

ERASED, rasyd. 15c., XVI 62, XXI 96 and 98, XXIV 113, XXV 118, XXVII 135. Torn off by the roots leaving a jagged edge (by derivation more properly 'eraced', French 'arraché', eradicated).

ERMINE. 13c., VII 26, IX 41, XI 46, XII 50 and 55, XIII 60, XV 64, XXII 99, 105, XXIV 113 and 116, XXVIII 140. Argent powdered with small black spots of conventional form varying with the period, representing the fur of the ermine.

ERMINES, erminees. 16c., XV 64. Ermine reversed. Sable powdered with argent. The treatise attributed to Nicholas Upton, c. 1440 or earlier (ed. Bysshe, 1654, p. 167), refers, with some disapproval, to the name 'hermynee' for such fields.

ESCALLOP. 13c., p. xviii, 40, XIII 59, XVI 66, XVII 71 and 74, XX 90, XXIV 110, 131, 133.

ESCHEQUETÉ, see Chequy.

ESCUCHEON, escutcheon, escochen. IV 18, VII 33, XV 64. A shield. Escucheon of pretence, p. xx. Inescocheon, XXIII 109, XXV 118, XXVI 122 and 126, XXVIII 142; a shield within a shield.

ESTOILE. 13c., p. xviii, (39), XVII 75, 88, XXI 95, XXVII 128, Star (q.v.). In early heraldry often interchangeable with the mullet, (104).

EXTERNAL ORNAMENTS, pp. XVI-XVII.

FALSE, faux. 13c. In early heraldry. Hollow or Voided (q.v.).

FER DE MOLINE, Millrind. 13c., p. xviii, VII 26. The iron which supports the upper millstone. The early form, shown in VII 26, later gave place to others, and itself came to be called Cross Moline.

FESS, fesse, fece. 13c., 12, VIII 34 and 38, XI 46, 68, XVI 69, 73, XVII 75 and 76, 77, 82, XXI 97, XXII 99 and 100, XXIII 103, 106, 111, 114, XXIV 120, XXVIII 140. Broad horizontal band across the middle of the shield (Latin, fascia, band). In fess, VIII 34 and 36, XI 46, XII 49,

XVII 71, XXVII 130, XXVIII 142. Per fess, XIV 63, XIX 82.

FIELD, p. xviii. Of the field, 40, XVI 65, XXI 96, XXII 99, XXIII 109, XXV 117 and 118. Of the same tincture as the field. See Repetition, avoidance of.

FIMBRIATED. 15c., XXV 118. Having a narrow edge or border of such a tincture (Latin, fimbria, thread or fringe).

FIRST, of the. 16c., XVI 65, XVII 78, 111, XXVI 122 and 125, (129), XXVIII 139 and 142. Of the first tincture named. See Repetition, avoidance of.

FITCHY, fitché, fixabyll. 14c. Of a cross, having the base sharpened so that it could be *fixed* in the ground. Cross paty fitchy, 15c., XII 51, XVII 71, 88, XXVI 124. Cross crosslet fitchy, 137

FLAG. XIX 82, XXV 117, XXVIII 141.

FLEUR DE LYS, fleur de lis, flurette, flure, flower de luce. 13c., p. xviii, VI 28, IX 41, XII 50 and 52, 53, XIII 61, XVI 69 and 70, XXI 96, XXIV 113, XXVI 125.

FLORY, fleury, flurette. 13c., VI 28, IX 41, XXVIII 136. Powdered with fleurs de lys. Cross florete, flourte, 13c., modern fleurettée, XXVI 125. The modern cross flory, XXV 117, perhaps from Late 14c.

FLORY COUNTERFLORY, flourete countre. 15c., I 2, V 27.

FORMY. 16c. Of a cross, with spreading arms; in modern heraldry interchangeable with Paty, q.v.

Fox, head of a. XXIV 113.

FRETTY, frette. 13c., VII 31, XI 46. A pattern of interlacing diagonal bands (Italian, ferrata, grating, from Latin, ferrum, iron). A Fret in modern heraldry, is a single pair of such bands interlaced with a mascle.

FRUCTED. XXII 100, XXIII 109, XXVIII 141. Having fruit of such a tincture.

FUR. Gerard Legh, 1562, classes together, Ermine, Argent, three more differently tinctured variants of Ermine, Verrey (i.e. Vair), and two variants of Vair, as 'nine sundry furres, which in scocheons are called by ix

107

proper names, and in mantels, they are called dowblinges'. This somewhat awkward grouping has been followed and indeed carried further in subsequent text books.

FURCHÉ. 13c. (7). Of a cross, having the arms forked into two, much as in the mediaeval Fer de Moline.

FUSIL. 14c., VIII 34, (43), XI 46, XVII 71. The spindle of a distaff (Latin, fusus, fusillus) conventionally represented as a lozenge. In modern heraldry (from c. 1390) distinguished from the lozenge, being made narrower and more pointed.

GAMB. 17c. or 18c., XXIV 119. A beast's leg. 'Paw', occurs much earlier.

GARB. 13c., III 11, 24, XV 64, 68, 92, XXVII 128. Wheatsheaf (old word obsolete except in heraldry).

GARTER. XV 64, XIX 82, XXII 99, XXV 118. The Garter Stall Plates (p. xxiii) show the arms of the Knights of the Garter encircled by the Garter from about 1500. As early as 1431, however, Sir William Bruges, Garter King of Arms displayed a Crown within a Garter on his seal.

GARTER KING OF ARMS, p. xxi. The King of Arms of the Order of the Garter and Principal King of Arms of English men, instituted by Henry V in 1417.

GARTER, Order of the. The principal and oldest English Order of Knighthood, founded by Edward III, probably in 1348.

GEMELS. 13c. p. xviii. A pair of closely adjacent barrulets (Latin, gemellus, twin).

GOBONY. 13c. (2), XI 46, XII 52, XIII 61, XXVII 127 Divided into rectangular sections (Gobon, gobbon, a slice ? = gobbet or French copon, coupon from couper, to cut).

GORGED. 17c., VI 28, XXII 99 and 100. Collared, having a collar, of such a tincture (from Gorge, throat), Ducally gorged, XXV 118, Collared with a ducal coronet.

GRANT OF ARMS. p. xxi.

GRITTY. p. xviii. The Boke of St. Albans, 1486 (ed. Dallaway, 1793, p. lxxviii) uses this as an inclusive term for the Repetitive Subdivisions (q.v.) of the field, Chequy, Undy (i.e. Barry wavy) and Vair. It seems to mean 'grated', 'like a grating'. The grouping together of Vair and certain Powdered fields (q.v.) as Furs (q.v.) I have not found earlier than Gerard Legh's 'Accedens of Armory', 1562.

GULES. 13c. Red.

GYRON, giron, geron. 13c. A triangular sector of a shield. (Old French, giron, a triangular piece, gusset, cognate with Gore.)

GYRONNY, gerone. 13c., VII 33, (116). Divided into gyrons. A gyronny shield in early heraldry has usually 12 gyrons. In modern heraldry the number is specified, as 'Gyronny of eight'.

HAND. XIX 82, XXVI 122 and 126.

HARP. XVIII 81.

HART. XXII 99.

HELMET. It is a solecism in modern heraldry to display a crest without its supporting helmet, if the shield is shown also. The system of restricting different forms of helmet to different ranks first began to appear in England under Elizabeth and became prevalent under James I. The Sovereign has a golden barred helmet shown full face, XVIII 81; Peers have a like helmet, but silver (but for the bars) and sidelong, XIX 82, XXII 99 and 100, XXV 117 and 118; Baronets and Knights have a helmet without bars shown open and full faced; and Esquires and Gentlemen have it without bars, closed and sidelong (as in XV 64).

HERALD. p. xiv.

HIND. XVI 65.

HOLLY. XXVIII 136.

HORSE, head of a, XXI 96, XXVII 135.

IMPALEMENT, as a method of marshalling, p. xix, IV 18, (41), XII 51, XIII 61, XVI 66, XVII 71, 88. See also Office, Arms of.

INDENTED, endente. 13c., I 1, II 5, (57), XIX 82, 91. Having the edge cut into with a continuous succession of toothlike angular incisions (Latin, indentatus, from, dens, tooth). In early heraldry the indentations are much deeper than in modern, so that what would now be blazoned *Three lozenges* or *fusils in fess,* in VIII 34, could then be blazoned *a fess indented* or *engrailed* (q.v.), these two terms also being then interchangeable.

INESCOCHEON. See Escocheon.

INVECTED. 16c., XXVIII 140. Notched into a succession of convexities, the opposite of Engrailed, q.v. But in earlier heraldic treatises (c. 1390-1486), Invecta, Inveckyt, is used as a synonym for Vair.

ISSUANT. XXV 117, but the same word as Jessant, q.v.

JESSANT DE LYS. IV 17, XXVII 134. Sprouting forth fleurs de lys. 14c. 'yssaunt', issuant, (17).

KING of ARMS. Originally (13c.) King of Heralds of Arms, King of Heralds, i.e. a principal or presiding herald.

LABEL. 13c., VI 28, IX 41 and 43, XI 46, XII 50. Used as a difference, sometimes of three, sometimes of five points. As the cadency mark of an eldest son in his father's lifetime, XXIII 104, it has three points which often taper towards the top.

LANGUED. XX 89. Having the tongue of such a tincture. Before the 16th century the tongues of beasts would be so tinctured as to stand out, but without mention in the blazon.

LAST, of the. XXVII 134. Of the last tincture named. See Repetition, avoidance of.

LEGATINE CROSS. XIV 63. The cross of a papal legate.

LEOPARD, lupar. 13c., p. XVIII, III 13, VI 28, VIII 36, IX 41, XII 50 and 52, 53, XIII 61, XVI 66 and 70. Since the 16th century generally blazoned Lion passant guardant (q.v.), and in treatises still earlier (c. 1390) Lion passant, Leo peditans. The old name, however, has always been kept for a Leopard's face (or head, teste de lupar), IV 17, VIII 38, XIV 63, 85, XXVII 134. The crest, VI 28, though adapted

to his position and shown as a Lion statant, would certainly have been blazoned Leopard, but cp. XVIII 81.

LILY. XIII 60. Henry VI's grant of arms to Eton College made in 1449 distinguishes the lilies as 'liliorum flores' from the fleur de lys, 'Francorum flore'.

LION. 13c. In early heraldry a Lion without qualification means a lion rampant; the Passant and Salient varieties also occur; the rest are 16c.

Lion passant. 13c., XIII 57, XIV 63, XVII 74, XXVIII 138

Lion passant guardant. 16c., XVII 76, XXVIII 141, in early heraldry called Leopard, q.v.

Lion rampant. 13c., p. XVIII, I 1 and 2, II 8, III 9 and 15, IV 18, 19, 23, V 27, IX 43, X 45, XII 54, XIII 56, XVI 65 and 69, XVII 71, XVIII 81, XIX 82, XX 89, XXI 95, XXIV 110, 112, XXIV 116, XXV 118, XXVII 130 and 132.

Lion rampant guardant. 16c., XVIII 81, XXII 100.

Lion rampant reguardant. 16c., XXV 117.

Lion sejant. V 27.

Lion sejant guardant. XIX 82.

Lion statant, (27), (28), see Leopard.

Lion statant guardant. XVIII 81.

Lion's gamb. XXIV 119. Lion's head, XXI 98. Demi-lion, XXV 118.

LIONCEL. 13c., III 9, IV 21. A little lion; term often used when several lions occur in a shield.

LOZENGE. 13c., VIII 34, XX 80, 94, XXIII 103. A rhombus, diamond shaped figure. See also Fusil, Mascle. 16c., used for a maid's or widow's arms in place of a shield, p. XX, XXIV 119.

LOZENGY, Lozengé. 16c. (the earlier term being Mascally, q.v.), III 14, XIII 60.

LUCY, luce, lucie. 13c. (43), IX 48.

LURE, conjoined in. XVI 70. From the conventional heraldic Hawk's lure, consisting of two wings, points down and joined above.

LYON KING OF ARMS. p. XXIII. The King of Arms of Scotland; named from the lion in the arms of that kingdom; mentioned 1420.

109

Man, bust of a. xxii 99: head of a (savage), xxviii 136.

Mantling. 15c., xv 64, xviii 81, xix 82, xxii 99 and 100, xxv 117 and 118. The conventional scroll work attached to the helmet, representing drapery actually worn for protection against the sun, i 2, v 27, vi 28, x 45, xi 46. Generally of a colour lined or doubled with a metal, though in early examples this is sometimes reversed, and Powdered, Gritty and even charged fields are sometimes substituted for one or other. Before the 16th century the choice of tinctures seems capricious. A fashion then came in for Gules and Argent, or Gules and Ermine for peers above the rank of baron, which lasted until the early 18th century when it gave place to the modern practice by the which the wreath (q.v.) and mantling are of the first metal and the first colour of the shield. There were always, however, numerous exceptions to the Gules and Argent custom, other tinctures often being specified in patents of arms. The form of mantling has varied greatly with time and the caprice of artists.

Marshalling. pp. xix-xx.

Martlet, merlett, merlot. 13c., p. xviii, iv 25, vii 30, xii 54, xiii 61, 68, xvi 69, xxviii 136 and 142. A conventional small bird usually shown without feet (the early form Merlot is a diminutive of French merle, from Latin, merula, blackbird; in the 16c., however, this was superseded by the form Martlet, properly meaning a Martinet or small martin). As the cadency mark of a fourth son, xxviii 136.

Mascle. 13c., synonymous with lozenge, q.v. (Latin, macula, mesh). In modern heraldry (perhaps from c. 1390), xxvi 122. A voided lozenge, 13c. 'Mascle voyde', 'faux lozenge'. Mascally, mascule, 13c. (14), the modern Lozengy.

Maunch, manche. 13c., p. xviii, xxiv 115. Conventional representation of a sleeve (Latin, manica, from manus, hand).

Metal. 15c., p. xvii. The metallic tinctures, Or and Argent.

Molet, see Mullet.

Moline, cross, see Fer de Moline.

Moorcock. xvi 67.

Motto. 16c., xiv 63, xv 64, xvii 75, xviii 81, xix 82, xxii 99 and 100, xxv 117 and 118. Word or short sentence shown generally on a scroll, above or more commonly below a coat of arms, but not forming part of it, and chosen at will by the individual bearer; probably originating in the 15c. display of Devises or War cries in this manner.

Mount. v 27, xxiii 109, xxvi 124, xxviii 141.

Mullet, molet, mole. 13c., p. xviii, vii 32, viii 39, 83, 106, xxvi 122 and 125, 129, 131. Conventional representation of a Spur rowel or revel, xxviii 139 (13c. rouel), sometimes pierced, (58), with a round hole; generally with 5, but sometimes with 6 points, xxviii 140; in early heraldry interchangeable with Star, estoile, xxiii 104. As cadency mark of a third son, (58), xxi 95, xxiii 103 (within an annulet), 111, xxv 118, xxvii 128, xxviii 138.

Natural charges, p. xviii.

Nebuly, innebulatyt. 15c., xxvii 134. With a wavy edge of peculiar form conventionally representing clouds.

Norroy King of Arms. p. xxi. King of Arms of England North of the Trent; mentioned 1338, but 'Petrus Rex heraldorum citra aquam de Trente ex parte boreali', mentioned 1276, presumably held this office. (Roy des Norreys, King of the North countrymen.) Under the Lancastrian Kings this office seems to have been held by Lancaster King of Arms.

Oak, slip of. xxii 100.

Office, arms of. p. xix. Anstis, Register of the Garter, Vol. I, p. 455, quotes what looks like an early example dated 1355.

Or. 12c. Gold or yellow. From the first appearance of English blazon in the fifteenth century till the early seventeenth century the use of Gold for Or and Silver for Argent was prevalent. They are still used for avoidance of repetition (see Repetition, avoidance of), and are indeed preferred for general use by Mr. Oswald Barron (The Ancestor, No. 1, p. 46), Gerard Legh (Accedens of Armory, 1562, fo. 1b) writes thus on the use of Or: 'L. That woorde is French and wherfore do ye blase in that language. G. I blase not in that language. But the termes of blasonne are in that language.'

ORANGE TREE. XXVIII 141.

ORDINARY. (1) 16c., p. xviii. Inclusive name for certain linear figures. Gerard Legh, 1562, classes as 'honorable ordinaries', the Cross, Chief, Pale, Bend, Fess, Escucheon, Chevron, Saltire and Bar (with their diminutives), and as 'Ordinaries general', the Gyron, Orle, Pile, Quarter, Canton and Flaunch.
(2) Ordinary of arms. 17c., pp. xxv, xxviii, xxix. Index of arms arranged by subject matter. The Oxford English Dictionary derives from a misunderstanding by Withy of Glover's title 'Book of Ordinaries'. An older term was Book of Suits.

ORLE, urle. 13c., VII 30. A border (diminutive of Latin ora, shore). This use still survives in the terms 'In orle', 'Orle of martlets', XXVIII 136 and the like. But Orle from the 16c., has meant a band parallel with but not touching the edge of the shield, IV 18, XXVI 122, XXVIII 136, for which the 13c. name was 'faux escochon', voided escucheon, and the 15c. 'Trace', tract. (See Tressure.)

OSTRICH FEATHER. VI 28.

OTTER. XXVI 124.

OVER ALL. VII 31, XI 46.

OX. XXVII 132.

PALE. 14c., IX 48, XXVIII 141. Vertical band. In pale, 88, XXIII 102, XXVII 127. Per pale, see Party per pale.

PALY, pale. 13c., VII 33, 73. Divided into a number of pales, in modern heraldry always and in early heraldry usually a specified even number.

PALL. XII 51, XVII 71, 88. A vestment conferred by the Pope on Archbishops and others.

PALM tree, palm branch. XXV 117.

PALMER'S STAFF. XVII 74.

PARTY. 13c., party per pale, per pale. I 1, II 8, IV 16 and 18, 23, IX 42, XII 51, XIII 61, XVI 65 and 66, XIX 82, 84, 88, XXV 118. See also impalement. Party of six pieces, XVI 69, 15c. 'escu de six pointz', modern blazon, Per fess of such tinctures a pale counterchanged.

PATENT OF ARMS. p. xxi.

PATONCE, Cross. 16c. (7). Modern name for the mediaeval Cross paty, q.v. (perhaps from Patentem for paty).

PATY, pate, pattée. 13c., II 7. In early heraldry a cross with extremities shaped like paws (French patte, paw, cf. Godefroy). By c. 1390 however false etymology had made it 'Crux patens', i.e. with opening or spreading arms, and straight ends. This form (otherwise called Formy, q.v.) appears, but with the base Fitchy (q.v.) in XII 51, XVII 71, 88, XXVI 124.

PELICAN. XVI 69, XVII 71.

PENNANT. XXV 118. Mistaken nautical form of 'Pennon', a long narrow pointed flag. When a knight bachelor was made banneret (q.v.), the pennon on his lance was turned into a banner by having the point cut off.

PHEON, feon. 15c., XVII 72. A broad arrow-head.

PIERCED. XII 51, (58).

PILE, pel. 13c., VIII 35, XVI 70, XXVIII 141. A wedge shaped figure, issuing, when there is only one and no other position is specified, from the chief (Latin pilum, javelin, hence, dart, arrow, spike).

PISTOL. XXV 117.

PLATE. 16c., XVI 65, (77), XXI 97, XXV 118. A roundel argent; earlier blazon, Torteau d'argent, Rondel d'argent, Pelott d'argent.

POINT. 15c. XVI 69, XVII 74. Portion of a shield cut off, especially (16c.) in base. Chief point, XXV 118. Points of a label. See Label.

POWDERED, poudre, or semé. 13c., V 27, VI 28, IX 41. Of a field, strewn with an indefinite number of some small charge; e.g. Flory, powdered with fleurs de lys: Crusilly, with crosses. Ermine with Ermines and its other variants logically belongs with the Powdered fields (cf. Fur).

PROPER. 15 or 16c., XIV 63, XVI 69, XVII 78, 88, XX 90, XXII 99 and 100, XXIII 109, XXV 117, XXVI 124, XXVII 128 and 130 and 134, XXVIII 136 and 138 and 139 and 140 and 141. Of the natural or proper colours.

PROPERTY IN ARMS, pp. xx-xxiii.

PURPURE, purple.

QUARTERLY, esquartele. 13c., II 3 and 6, VI 28, VII 31, VIII 39, IX 41, X 45, XI 46, 105, XXV 118. Originally and properly, divided into four quarters, but as Quartering (pp. xix-xx) comes into fashion, so Quarterly of six, eight and the like appears. Quarterings are numbered in horizontal rows beginning in chief, and in each row from dexter to sinister, VI 28, VIII 39, IX 41, XI 46, XII 50 and 52 and 54, 53, XIII 56 and 57 and 61, XV 64, XVI 66 and 69 and 70, XVIII 81, XIX 82, XX 90, XXIV 116, XXV 118, XXVI 122, 129, XXVII 132. Quarterly quartered, XI 46, means that a quartering is itself quartered. The Quarter as a charge is the dexter chief quarter if not otherwise specified.

QUATREFOIL. 16c., p. xviii (121). Conventional flower with four leaves.

QUEUE FOURCHÉE, cowe furche. 13c., I 1. With forked tail.

RAGGED STAFF. XI 46.

REPETITION, avoidance of. In the sixteenth century a fashion of blazon came in, whereby no term is used twice in one blazon if it can be avoided. Hence such phrases as: Of the field, the first, second, third, last (q.v.). As many XXVII 127, Like number XXVII 128, Gold for Or (q.v.), when Or has been already named.

REPETITIVE SUBDIVISIONS of the field, p. xviii. See Gritty.

REVERSED. IV 17. Upside down.

ROLLS OF ARMS, pp. xxiv-xxxi.

ROSE. 13c., IX 44, XIV 63, XVI 69, XX 79 and 90. In early heraldry roses and cinquefoils are interchangeable. The rose is shown in this conventional manner unless blazoned 'slipped' or 'stalked', when it appears in profile with a stalk.

ROUNDEL, rondel, ronde. 13c. In early heraldry Torteau (q.v.), Pelotte, were synonyms, the tincture, as d'argent, de gules, being always specified. In the sixteenth century, however, special names were given to roundels of the different tinctures. Bezant (Or), Plate (Argent), Torteaux (gules), Pellet (sable) and others.

SABLE. 13c. Black (perhaps from the fur of the sable, though this is brown. The common use of the word for 'black' derives from the heraldic.)

SAILOR. XXV 117.

SALTIRE, saltoir, sautoir, sautour, salter, saltier. 13c., V 27, XI 46, XIII 56, XVI 66, XX 79, XVIII 81, XX 87, XXV 118. (Latin saltatorium, a place for leaping, stile). The Crosses (q.v.) of St. Andrew and St. Patrick are Saltires. In saltire, saltier ways, saltirewise, XIV 63, XXI 101, XXV 118, XXVII 127, XXVIII 141. Per saltire, XXIV 116, XXV 118, XXVII 130, XXVIII 142.

SAVAGE'S HEAD. XXVIII 136.

SEALS, as evidence of arms, p. xxiii.

SECOND, of the. 16c., XI 51, XIII 60, XVII 71, XIX 82, XXIV 113, XXV 118, XXVI 122. Of the second tincture named. See Repetition, avoidance of.

SEEDED. IX 44, XIV 63, XVI 69, XX 90. Having seeds of such a tincture.

SEMÉ. See Powdered.

SERPENT. XXVIII 140.

SHELL, of a whelk. XXIV 120. See also Escallop.

SHIP. XXV 117.

SINISTER. c. 1390 (see Dexter). The wearer's left side of a shield, that is the spectator's right, XII 51, XV 64, 88, XXII 99, XXV 117, XXVI 122, XXVIII 141; later for left in general, XXVI 122 and 126.

SLIP OF OAK. XXII 100.

SLIPPED. XIII 60. Of a plant, torn off from the stem.

SPANISH FLAG. XXV 117.

SPEAR. XVII 78. Spear head 137.

SPHERE (75), XXI 95, XXIII 107.

SPUR REVEL. See Mullet.

STAFF. XXVIII 140.

STAG. XXII 100. Stag's head, XXVIII 139.

STAPLE. XII 55.

STAR, see Estoile. Polar star, XXIII 107.

STATANT. Standing in profile with all four feet on the ground. See Lion. Of an otter, XXVI 124; of an ox, XXVII 132.

STOCK, of an anchor. XXIII 102.

STORK. XXII 100.

SUPPORTERS, p. xvi, XIV 63, XV 64, XVIII 81, XIX 82, XXII 99 and 100, XXV 117 and 118.

SURMOUNTED BY. XII 51, XIV 63, XXV 117 and 118, XXVII 127, XXVIII 141.

THIRD, of the. 16c., XXIV 113, XXVII 127 and 128. Of the third tincture named. See Repetition avoidance of.

THISTLE. XXVIII 138.

THREE, TWO AND ONE. XVI 65. See Disposition of charges.

THROUGHOUT. XIX 82. Extending to the edges of the field.

THUNDERBOLT. XXVIII 139.

TINCTURE. 17c. pp. xvii-xviii. Inclusive term for the heraldic metals (q.v.) and colours (q.v.), and later also the furs (q.v.). The system of indicating tinctures by different hatchings appeared in Langrius' map of Brabant, 1600, and was popularized by the 'Tesserae Gentilitiae' of Silvester de Petra Sancta, 1638. In England it appears in 1649 on the seals in the engraving of the Death Warrant of Charles I.

TORTEAUX. 13c., a roundel, q.v. (French, tortel, torteau, a cake). 16c., a roundel gules, 77.

TOWER. XVI 65, XXVII 130.

TRAPPER, p. xvi, I 1 and 2, V 27, VI 28, X 45, XI 46.

TREE. XV 64, XIX 82. Cotton tree, XXIII 109.

TRESSURE. 16c., I 2, V 27. A narrow band parallel with the edge of the shield. From French tressure, a ribbon for binding the hair, tresses. The word has, however, assumed this form only through false etymology, the fifteenth century synonym (from which it is corrupted) being trace, tract, i.e. track. See also Orle.

TRICK. 16c. To indicate tinctures on a sketch of arms by their initial letters.

TRICOLOURED FLAG. XXV 117.

TRIPPANT, tripping. 16c., XVI 65. Of a beast, walking in profile with one foot off the ground.

TURKEY, p. xviii-xix.

TWO AND ONE. XXVI 126. See Disposition of Charges.

TYNE. XVI 66. Pointed branch of an antler.

ULSTER KING OF ARMS, p. xxii. The King of Arms of Ireland; instituted 1552. But Ireland King of Arms is several times mentioned between 1382 and 1477.

UNDULATED. XXV 117. Wavy.

UNGULED, ungled. 16c., XXII 99, XXVII 132. Having hoofs of such a tincture.

VAIR, verre, verrey. 13c., II 6, III 14, XVII 76. A conventional variegated (Latin varius, particoloured) pattern of field, the pattern of which varies at different periods; blue and white unless otherwise specified (when in modern heraldry it is called Vairy of such tinctures). The same word was applied in the Middle Ages to a variegated fur much used for lining garments, and it seems doubtful whether Vair in heraldry is a conventional representation of this or merely shares the same etymology.

VARIEGATED fields, p. xviii. See Gritty and Powdered fields.

VERT. 13c. Green.

VISITATIONS. Heralds'. p. xxii.

VOIDED, voyde. 13c., IV 18, XXVIII 142, hollowed out, earlier synonyms, faux 13c., percee 14c.

VOLANT. 16c., XXIII 109, XXVI 126. Flying.

WAVES of the sea. XXV 117.

WAVY. XVII 74 and 75, XXV 117. In early heraldry the 'waves' are much deeper.

WHELK SHELLS. XXIV 120.

WINGS. XVI 70.

WREATH. (1) or torse; 14c., XV 64, XIX 82, XXII 99 and 100, XXV 117 and 118; twisted band joining the crest to the helmet, generally tinctured as the mantling (q.v.).
(2) as a charge, XX 86.
(3) of laurel, XXVII 134.

WYVERN. 17c., X 45, XIX 82. Winged dragon with two legs only (earlier Wyver, i.e. Viper.)

INDEX